LOOKING BACK

and

DROPPING NAMES

This book is dedicated to my children Emma and Robin

LOOKING BACK

and

DROPPING NAMES

a memoir

by

Moray Watson

The Erskine Press
2016

LOOKING BACK and DROPPING NAMES

First Published 2016 by
The Erskine Press, The White House, Sandfield Lane, Eccles,
Norwich NR16 2PB

WWW.ERSKINE-PRESS.COM

Text © Moray Watson

Introduction © Dame Judi Dench

The moral right of the author has been asserted

A CIP catalogue record is available from the British Library

This edition © The Erskine Press

ISBN 978 1 85297 120 5

Typeset by Barkers Print & Design Ltd. Attleborough, Norfolk.
Printed and bound in Great Britain by Page Brothers Ltd. Norwich, Norfolk

Acknowledgements

Firstly I must thank my son, Robin for suggesting that I jolly well get on and write this book.

He then found Liz Flower whom I thank for kindly travelling from Wales to help me.

Thank you to Crispin de Boos for bravely taking on this project.

A huge thank you to Garen Robinson for arranging all the photographs and for his much appreciated computer wizardry.

Enormous gratitude to my brilliant daughter, Emma and her gallant husband, Rupert for putting it all together.

I would like to take this opportunity to thank all the people that I have mentioned in these pages and to sincerely apologise to those that I have failed to mention. You are not forgotten but treasured.

Contents

Foreword

"Looking Back and Dropping Names"

I have known Moray Watson for more years than either of us care to think about. The first time we worked together was in 1968 in a production of "On approval", with Maggie Smith and Robert Stephens. As far as I can remember, it was live television – something that is unheard of today. My one abiding memory of that play is Moray and me walking down a staircase. I was wearing a tartan cloche hat, which seemed to amuse Moray and eventually caused us both to corpse. I stopped in my tracks, and Moray tried to cover it up by tying his shoelace. I think we were both threatened with the sack!

Later in his career, my daughter Finty Williams was lucky enough to work with him in a 1999 production of "The Chiltern Hundreds", and they too became firm friends - so he is practically a member of my family!

I found his book a fascinating read, right from the first page when he says that his father was hoping for a girl so that he would not have the expense of educating her, but that was the era into which he was born. However, that did not stop him from becoming one of the most successful actors of his generation. Dropping names is a very apt title for a book but, in this case, Moray has worked with and knows all the "names" he has dropped.

Moray has indeed had a fascinating life and I have enjoyed my journey through the pages. He is the most gentle man I have ever known, with the most impeccable manners. I wish there were more like him!

1

Childhood, Sunningdale and London

My two earliest memories are not mine at all, but handed down to me, because, in essence, it is my story even if I was too young to have witnessed it. When I was born, on 25 June 1928 in a house in Sunningdale sometime in the morning, I was expected to be a girl. My parents, Gerry and Jean, already had two sons, my brothers Michael and Johnnie and the thought of another boy did not really seem to have been contemplated, mostly because my father did not want the expense of educating another boy. A girl, on the other hand, did not need to be educated; a bit of a governess for a while, a reasonable proficiency at the piano and then the art of running a house was deemed suitable for the life of a girl who was, anyway, her father's property until her husband came to claim her. So that was what was intended for me. But I upset the imagined future order of things by being a boy. My father was irritated, but not at that point incandescent. His fury came when his missed his usual train to London. That was probably the unforgiveable act.

The second hand-me-down memory comes at my christening. My father, when asked to attend, says that "this is nothing to do with me." I am christened – my names are Moray Robin Philip Adrian Watson. And this raises a question which has lain in the back of my mind all my life, occasionally coming to the fore as it does right now, and to which I don't have an answer. Why were my brothers, Michael and John, given three names each, all family names? My names, all four of them, on the other hand, seem random and unconnected. Someone did once suggest they were the names of my mother's lovers! Well – that may be. She was a beauty and I don't think she lacked in the "it" department. But the question of the names has always made me wonder and now of course it is too late to ask her. However, as it turned out, being called Moray has been a great advantage and very much a part of who I am as an actor.

The one concrete memory of Sunningdale is not of the house or my parents or my brothers but of Nanny Templeton. If I were to stage my memories as a play then the curtain would rise on an empty stage clad entirely in grey felt, featureless and dimly lit. A spot would come on – not entirely focussed – on a figure in a far corner. The face is left out of the light but the figure, which should be comfortably built, holds a child. I don't know how one would do the next bit, but the figure comes down stage and as she does, the child grows older and bigger until he is about six and then, in place of the grey felt box, there is a back projection of a nineteenth century Chelsea Street with a rag and bone man, a stop-me-and-buy-one and the bloke with the coal. The coal makes a heck of a racket as it is poured through the circular metal flaps in the pavement that lead to the coal cellar, the stop-me-and-buy-one has a hurdy gurdy calling all us boys to buy ice cream and the rag and bone man shouts "RAAAG'N'B'N, raaag'n'b'n, raaag'n'b'n" as he disappears around the corner. These are the sunny uplands of urban childhood. I learnt to ride my bicycle, I went to school.

We had moved to Chelsea; 13 Smith Street off the King's Road. I shared a room at the top of the house with my brother Johnnie. We shopped at Harrods from the No.19 or the 22 bus. My father created a much-admired alpine rock garden, all the current rage, in the garden. My mother had had the money to buy the house. I don't know what had happened to the place in Sunningdale, nor do I really know why my parents decided to move. I assume that they both wished to live in London. I know that my father had had enough of commuting from Sunningdale to Bond Street. And who would not wish to live in London in the 1930s? It was a tremendously exciting place to be.

John and Moray

My father worked for the family shipping company, Galbraith and Pembroke in South Molton Street. There were models of ships in the window of the business – made by my father. He was good with his hands and artistic in ways that are acceptable today but were not then. Working with your hands was not a gentlemanly thing to do. Years later I asked my mother what he would have liked to have done with his life. Without hesitation she responded that he should have been a landscape gardener. He designed all the gardens of all the houses they lived in and, aside from calling in friends for a wall-building party or something similar, he

Jean Watson

would dig and plant and earth-move himself. He really did not, apparently, enjoy working for the family business and when the war came in 1939 he signed up as an officer with the Royal Sussex regiment mostly, I suspect, because he was friendly with several of the officers who lived nearby. Up to that point he had been a Territorial in the Middlesex Yeomanry, but over the years had felt an overweening snobbery creep in – something that he did not care for. So the Royal Sussex became his regiment. But I get ahead of myself.

Gerald Arthur Watson in his Middlesex Yeomanry uniform

What I remember of Smith Street is Margaret, the maid and Lottie, the cook who had a lovely deep singing voice; my bedroom at the top of the house which I shared with Johnnie; learning to ride a bicycle; Harrods; Mr Smith, the cat; my father reading to us (just the once); my mother saying goodnight before going out; and school – Gibbs pre-preparatory school at the bottom of Sloane Street.

We used to shop in Harrods. Walking in from the street – we used the Hans Place entrance where the lifts were – was to walk through the looking glass. You moved from the bright dustiness of the outside through double doors, first into magic dimness then into a large airy space which smelt of expensive polish and manifold dreams. It was a feeling of excitement, contained and dampened by the intimate vastness of the place. Children did not shout or tug their minders, sandals squeaked on the floor while the heels of the women clicked and clacked over the marble.

We would head for the lifts – each lift dominated by a uniformed attendant. I never knew how they knew when to raise the lever that would make the lift stop at a floor – it looked like such a precise knowledge and that the operation of each lift turned the attendant into a scientific wonder. At each floor they would announce the full range: "Ladies fashions, ladies shoes, household linens, haberdashery" that would have been the first and second floors and then the third – "Children's clothes, children's shoes, children's toys and the Harrods Zoo". The last being of the hugest possible excitement.

But before the delight of the animals it would be shoe time. This was also fun in a slightly spectral way. Once a shoe attendant had been allocated, the first thing we had to do was put our feet into a large box, the x-ray box, wearing the shoes we came in. Then the attendant would peer in, one's mother would also look and some conversation would take place about the necessity of new shoes and if so what size would be best. And while they held this conversation (which was of minimal interest to me), I would look into the box. And there were my feet, except that I couldn't see my normal feet, I could see the bones, all lurid green and the edge of the shoes perhaps touching the edges of the bones, perhaps not. I could wiggle my toes and see my bones move, could see the effect on the rest of the bones in my feet when I did a toe wiggle. Magic stuff. It was always a bit of a let-down when I had to take my feet out of the box and pay attention to the boring question of new shoes.

But there was a reward: the Harrods zoo and the pet shop. Kittens and puppies, rabbits and chinchillas, rats and mice and reptiles and birds. There was a rustling and snuffling and cheeping and twittering and squeaking all around, mixed with a smell of sawdust and that peculiar warmth of young animal. Every cage was a delight. If I had had my way there would have been no room in Smith Street for anyone but me, possibly Margaret who was a constant in my life, and all the animals from Harrods Zoo.

And then came Mr Smith. My mother decided she wanted a cat. A Siamese kitten arrived from Harrods, all blue eyes and miaou. It was given some exotic oriental name by my mother and it died within a few days. Nothing daunted, my mother tripped off to Harrods and bought a second kitten – again given a pretty oriental name but this one also died within a few days. My father, to make sure that there was nothing my mother was doing wrong, decided they would both go to Harrods and choose a third Siamese kitten. My mother was not the only one who had had a kitten die: the whole litter had heart problems and so she was given a third one, with no charge. My father decided that he would name this one. They came back with this third kitten and told us that this cat would be called Smith, Mr Smith "… after the street we live in!". And Smith it was. Smith did not die and Smith was a delight.

When we moved to Petworth when the war broke out, Smith came with us and took to the country as if he were a farm cat. He would come out walking all day with the three of us, Michael with a 20 bore shot gun, Johnnie with a 4/10 and me with a long stick, about eighteen feet long, to poke at squirrel's drays – or anything else that took our fancy that we might shoot at. Smith just kept us company and did his own hunting and gathering. Every so often Smith would just stand still and I would hear a "whuh whuh

whuh" which meant "pick me up and carry me". I always did. He would drape himself around my neck and his whiskers would tickle my cheek and I could feel his purring as a thrum against my shoulder. And just as quickly he would decide he had enough and it would be time to leap off and return to hunting in the grass. Wonderful Mr Smith the cat-dog.

Smith Street was where I learned to ride my bicycle. Well, not exactly in the street – we, Johnnie and I, used to take our bicycles to Burton Court where a portly Chelsea Pensioner let us in and watched benignly while we skidded around on the cobbles. It was quite hard when we fell off, lots of grazes and knee and hand scrapes - but I soon learnt to stay upright. One of the reasons for going there was the old Pensioner – and goodness he did look old. He could have said he was as old as Noah and I would have believed him. I loved his uniform, too, the red overcoat, the black cap, the frogging. I thought it might be just the thing – to be a Chelsea pensioner.

I have two strong memory pictures of my parents while at Smith Street. One is of my mother coming into our bedroom to say goodnight before she went out to dinner. She would kiss us on our foreheads so as not to mess her makeup and tell us to be good boys, to not forget our prayers and to sleep well. I thought I had never seen anything so beautiful nor smelt anything quite so fragrant. And it is not just the boy remembering his mother as beautiful – she was a beauty, as some of my photographs show. She had elegance and poise and always looked quite stunning when she was dressed up to go out. Wafting is a cliché, I know, but she did waft and her perfume wafted with her. She had a penchant for the theatre and in fact spent two terms at RADA. Both she and my father were quite heavily involved with the local amateur dramatic society when they lived in Sunningdale. Who knows what sort of an actress she would have made? The life of one, providing it was a glamorous life, would have suited her. If I extend my imagination a bit further, I can just glimpse her as a film star, feted and.... wafting.

The one memory of my father that stays with me is of his reading to all three of us in the evening before we went to bed. He never came up to our bedroom. Not his kind of place at all. Instead this memory has him reading to us downstairs as we sit on the floor round his huge armchair. He read from a book titled "The Amateur Gentleman" by Jeffrey Farnol. I understood not one word but that is not the point. I was only 6 years old! It generated a feeling, for that half hour, of closeness and I felt safe in that cocoon. In every other respect both he and my mother were essentially somewhat distant. She was good on manners and the proper way to be and behave. At meals how to hold a knife and fork and a soup spoon. To stand up if a lady comes into the room. To walk on the outside of a pavement when walking down the street. To call any man who was over twenty-one "Sir". We said our prayers every night:

"Gentle Jesus meek and mild
Look upon a little child
Pity my simplicity (although I would say "pity mice and pity me")
Suffer me to come to thee
God bless Mummy and Daddy, Michael and Johnnie, Grandpapa and Kinki, (I will explain who she was later), Margaret and Lottie and everyone I love.
Through Jesus Christ Our Lord
Amen"

But manners and good behaviour notwithstanding, truthfully I do not remember much affection from them to any of us. The affection and attention we needed came from Margaret.

Then there was Sabu. In 1937 the film "Elephant Boy" came to the cinema down the road. The star of this film was Sabu (Sabu Dagastir). It was a thrilling film, exotic and different, passionate and foreign. I watched with my knuckles in my mouth as the elephant picked Sabu up with his trunk. Surely, I thought, that large unwieldy trunk would crush the life out of Sabu. But no. The unwieldiness turned into pure delicacy as it curled round Sabu and lifted him up so carefully, so tenderly to place him behind the elephant's ears. And there he sits, master of his world, riding this massive swaying creature which then ambles with such delicacy through the jungle. It was a wonderful film; the sort of film that makes your imagination sway and conjure up mysteries. Sabu was such a star.

Then came the day when Margaret took me on a No. 19 bus to Harrods. I was wearing my school uniform, I think, shorts and the Gibbs school cap and maroon blazer. We were going to see Sabu, the young Indian actor. Looking back, he was obviously on a public relations trip but for me I knew nothing of publicity and its infernal round – I was going to meet a slice of magic. We took the lift to the third floor. I took my cap off in the lift, all gentlemen removed their hats in a lift, I forget why, and were ushered into a quite big room, that was obviously used for lectures and visiting dignitaries, probably with about 50 seats in it, ranged in theatre style. It was designed to look like a cosy gentleman's library with oak bookshelves and desks. We took our seats. There was the usual hum of expectation, the waves of which died away and then rose again as Sabu came in and sat in a chair next to a table on a little dais. I'm sorry to say that I do not remember if he spoke – or if anyone said anything. I suppose someone must have introduced him, I suppose people clapped, I suppose he did speak. I remember how he looked, in a coat of silver brocade and a turban of saffron and his olive face, dark eyes and lovely smile. I remember going up to the dais and shaking his hand and on a visiting card he wrote SABU in large curling letters and I remember thinking how beautiful, how quite beautiful he was. It was one of those occasions which is very small in the scheme of things, but very large in a boy's life at the time and the kind of occasion that is held as a treasure in the virtual box of memories that make up a life. Seeing Sabu in *Elephant Boy* and meeting him in Harrods were one of the two things that crystallised what I wished to do with my life.

The other was a trip to the theatre at the end of one particular holiday, a few years later, to see a play. My mother had the habit of taking us once at the beginning and once at the end of the holidays so it was a part of our upbringing to go to the theatre. In fact the theatre-going public was quite a large proportion of the public in general as there were few other distractions, no television for instance. I loved going to the theatre – the ability to lose oneself in a story, the anticipation at the dimming of the lights, the quieting of the audience, the gentle rustles as people settled.... and then it is like a collective intake of breath as the curtains open. The excitement has never gone. I experience exactly the same feelings now as I did when I was ten.

We moved out of London to Petworth in Sussex quite soon after the war started though my parents must have continued to use the Smith Street house for London trips. Anyway, at some point during the conflict, a bomb fell a street or two away. The reverse pressure wave of the bomb, rather like a backdraft in a fire, caused the outer wall in our bedroom to bow outwards; it just sucked bricks out, forming what was known as a "bomb bulge". Years later I met Toby Rowland, the theatrical impresario, who, it turned out, had later bought the house. I asked him if there was still a bomb bulge in one of the rooms on the top floor. Much to my amusement he nearly fainted with surprise; "How did you know?" Indeed, how would a stranger know about such a thing? He rectified it – although it wasn't strictly necessary, and apparently it cost him more in scaffolding than my mother had paid for the house. That also amused me.

2

Petworth, Prep School and Eton College 1939-1946

Sometime during my prep school years we moved to the country. My father found a house called Wickers on the Kirdford Road two miles eastward from Petworth in Sussex. It was surrounded by woodland, a paradise for boys. It was not a particularly big house but it was pretty and there was a large garden which my father completely remodelled. He planted herbaceous borders which was very much the new garden fashion. He built walls and planted trees. He continued to travel to London for work, and he fulfilled his duties as a Captain in the Royal Sussex Regiment. It seems, in retrospect, that he was there for far longer than he actually was. My memory has him catching the train daily, but it also has him digging the garden and inviting friends for bricklaying parties. Everyone was given a job to do and it had to be executed just so. It was just an extension of his military manoeuvres.

We did have a gardener, Kenward, who doubled as chauffeur. I have no idea what his Christian name was. Kenward was 5ft 2 and my father was 6ft 4. They were an odd couple pottering around the gardens. My father would drive Kenward to the station at Pulborough to catch the train to the regimental barracks. Then Kenward would come back from the station to take my mother shopping. I can see him, head just visible, in chauffeurs cap, behind the enormous steering wheel peering between the top of the wheel and the dash - looking as if he was hunkered down when in reality he was sitting normally. I dread to think what the range of his visibility was. He was fast but he was good. The car was a Buick, big, smart, solid, with a bull nose and headlights too close together. It was an upmarket purposeful car with whitewall tyres. Very much the fashion of the time. And my father had a passion for cars. As well as the Buick he once had a Studebaker and a Ford V8. When my father was eventually sent abroad with the British Expeditionary Force, Kenward's name became used as a code in his letters to her. In this way he kept her informed of where he was in Northern France.

We three boys got thoroughly involved with country life in the holidays – including the squirrel hunting with Mr Smith. We cycled everywhere in

Sussex. No other way to get around. I remember one Christmas Johnnie's present sitting in the drawing room – a brand new shiny black elegant road bike. I have no idea what make it was, nor do I know what make mine was, but it wasn't as gleamingly black and shiny as Johnnie's. If we weren't on our bicycles we seemed to spend days in the woods and in the fields. Today, when there is a particular kind of autumn morning, misty but with a sharp clear blue sky above, the kind of morning where scents travel, I am taken back to the mornings when we would get up at 6, don caps and boots and head out with the hunt to go cub hunting.

The days meld and I could be standing at the edge of the wood, waiting. We were always on foot, and the wood that the hounds were casting in would be surrounded not only by those on horses but those of us on foot as well. We would be spread out about 30 feet apart, all turned towards the wood, concentrating on the sounds, watching for a brown face with beady eyes. And the brief was to make a noise to turn any fox, any cub, back into the wood. Under no circumstances were we to relax our vigilance, or allowed to let a fox escape. Any sign, any rustling, and we would holler and thwack our sticks against our boots to frighten the animal back into the woods. You would hear the "come up, come up" of the huntsman and whips, then the occasional encouragement of the horn, just a short upward toot. And then you would hear the hounds sing and you would know they were on the scent. Once, however, a pair of black-tipped ears and bright enquiring eyes poked his sharp nose out right in front of me. The watcher to my left was out of sight and the one to my right was concentrating into the wood. I had a choice.

Well, actually, I did not have a choice. I saw no reason why I should send the cub back. I stood aside, shooed him past me and watched him go, low to the ground, tail streaked out behind. There was just a moment while I held my breath in case any of the nearer watchers spotted him, but no. He was safely gone. I would have been "for it" in no uncertain terms if he had been seen: easy to find out who had been lax. And to be lax while a watcher out cubbing was not the done thing.

We were friends with the children of Lord and Lady Leconfield, the owners of Petworth House. Lady Leconfield was quite marvellously eccentric; her letterhead was simply "Lady Lec, Pet, Sus.". He was quite frightening, particularly to small boys. She, Violet, was tall and willowy. He was not. We knew him as Lordy. Not to his face, of course. I don't think he knew what to say to boys so we crossed his path as little as we could. When I think of

Violet I see her standing on top of a jeep, behatted, opening a fete in the grounds of Petworth House. She was wearing apricot slacks. She was very tall and to a small boy her head seemed almost to be in the clouds. Violet was remarkably kind to my mother, especially after my father died.

I used to spend quite some time with their son, Peter Wyndham. He and his sister Elizabeth were adopted which meant that Peter would not inherit the title. This moved sideways to Lordy's younger brother. Of the two it would be Elizabeth who would be upset about this. She was immensely social and lived the life. Peter on the other hand was not entirely comfortable with it. I remember once, cubbing, when I was being a foot soldier at the edge of a copse, Peter came up to me on his white pony (which we called grey) and offered me a ride. I don't think he really enjoyed it. I would have loved to get on his pony but I would have been severely ticked off for doing so. I was, on the whole, a very good and obedient boy. I was well aware of "appearances" and the censure if you stepped out of place. There were those that didn't give a fig about those things, my brother Johnnie being one of them, but really it was much easier to abide by the rules - written or unwritten.

I was sent to Allen House, Hook Heath near Woking in September 1935. I was 7. Johnnie was there too. Michael had already started at Eton. Michael had been sent to a prep school in Herefordshire. He did not stay. Tales of paedophilia reached my grandfather and he was removed. I was still at Allen House at the start of the war. I was in the sickroom in isolation at the top of the house. I had acute earache and was there for a whole term. I used to enjoy looking out over the countryside towards London twenty-five miles away. At night I could see the general glow from the city that lit the night sky. I imagined all those people going about their business just as we used to do. From a distance I felt like a puppet master, that my thoughts could influence who was doing what.

One night I said to Matron – who had come to settle me down for the night: "There's a very big glow over London tonight, much brighter than usual" Matron" Don't be silly, dear, that's just normal. Go to sleep." Me "No it isn't, its much, much brighter than usual. What is it?" Matron: "Do go to sleep dear, I promise you it's quite normal". I did go to sleep but I knew it wasn't usually as bright as that at night. The next morning Matron came in and said "I have to apologise to you, Moray. You were quite right. I heard on the wireless that The Crystal Palace was in flames." For me this is unforgettable for two reason: one that an adult apologised, unheard of in my book and two: the burning of such a beautiful and historic building was certainly breath-taking in the real sense – you do catch your breath in thinking about it and remembering just how fabulous it was. Such a feat of engineering, such beauty and gone in a puff. It was thrilling to watch and I was the only boy in the whole school who saw it!

In 1940, in the early spring, we spent six weeks at Long Burton near Sherbourne in Dorset in a cottage next to where my father was stationed with the 4th Battalion of the Royal Sussex Regiment. My mother, my two brothers and I were all down there in a cottage next door to Colonel Lashmere Whistler, his wife and two daughters, Penelope and Jennifer. The highlight of those six weeks was a Camp Concert in which we were all encouraged to join in the singing of the Regimental Song "Sussex By The Sea." When the Battalion left Long Burton, Johnnie and I marched with them on the side of the road as they made their way to Sherbourne station before going on to Southampton and thence to Northern France. This was, of course, only a few months after the start of the Second World War and the regiment had no idea where or when they would encounter the German army.

As it turned out they had to march for many days across Northern France without a shot being fired. One of the Royal Sussex officers found this particularly tiring; Bernard Fitzalan-Howard, the 16th Duke of Norfolk, a major. He went to see the Medical Officer and confessed to him that there was gout in the family and he must have inherited it. The MO said that he would arrange for Bernard to go into Transport. Bernard replied that it was out of the question – "he would be ridiculed by his Company" – and that "I must carry on marching." The MO reported the situation to the Colonel who told Bernard that he was a liability and that he would arrange for his return to England. Poor Bernard rather dreaded headlines in the English press such as "Senior Duke Returns to England with Gout". But the moment he was back in England, in Dover, he bought a newspaper to discover that there was racing in Brighton. He made his way over there, pretty sure that he would find his wife at the races. He was right. She was!

In 1940, May 21st to be exact, my father was killed in Belgium. My mother delegated the task of telling Johnnie and me to Dee Goody, who was my mother's best friend from Byworth. I loved Dee. Michael told me some time ago that I always put on a different voice when talking about her. I had no idea. But truthfully I felt closer to her than my mother and in some ways loved her a great deal more. So my mother went to Eton to tell Michael, and

Dee, who looked rather like Margaret Rutherford, came to Allen House where Johnnie and I were called to the headmaster's drawing room. It was a big room with oriental carpets and it seemed to me we stood in the middle of a vast space and Dee came in. "My dears," she said, "I have some awful news and you must be brave". I had no idea what was to come but it felt like the walls were receding and I was getting smaller. "Your father," she went on, looking at me, looking at Johnnie and back to me. She paused and began again. Her voice was very emotional, trembly, low and dramatic. "Your father has been dreadfully badly wounded". Her manner was very affecting, in the true sense of the word. I could feel the terror of it. "He has a bad wound and is very unwell". I could feel tears and blinked heavily to keep them away. But Johnnie and I went back to our lessons and for the moment that was that.

Apparently when Dee returned to my mother she was asked what had been said. Dee told my mother that she had taken one look at "Moray's poor little face, with his eyes blurred with tears" and could not face telling him. "So what did you say?" Asked my mother. "I told them both that Gerry had been badly wounded and was very unwell." She confessed to not being able to say any more. My mother rang the school and asked the headmaster to tell us the truth of the matter. His method of telling me was to hand me the death notice from The Times.

I don't remember that he said anything. I do remember a kind of shifting of the earth, a slipping sideways, the sense that nothing would ever be the same again. I was desperately upset about the loss of my father, a man I did not really know and who had only just begun to develop a sort of closeness with Michael, now that Michael was approaching adulthood. That would have come with Johnnie and me in time, of course it would. But for the moment there was a deep sadness for the loss of my father, because he was my father.

Years later, I wanted to see where he was killed. I called the War Office who were very helpful, gave me routes, the whole works, buses, trains everything. I got off the bus in Anzegem at the same time as a woman and a boy of about 6 or 7. I asked her the way to the graves of the English soldiers killed in the 2nd Great War. She started to give me directions but the lad interrupted and said if it were the English officers then the way was up in the huge Belgian cemetery. I found the grave, one among many identical stones saying simply Captain GA Watson, 4th Battalion Royal Sussex Regiment, beloved husband of Jean, father of Michael, John and

Moray. It was a pilgrimage for me to see the grave and gave me a tremendous feeling of peace. I have been again with Emma, my daughter, and my son-in-law Rupert. Again this was incredibly moving. We arrived and, as before when I had visited, there were fresh flowers on the grave almost as if they had been ordered in advance for our visit. It is a strange place to feel love but that's exactly what it was.

My father, Gerry Watson, had gone to France with the British Expeditionary Force in 1940. He was a Captain commanding D company in the 4th Battalion of the Royal Sussex Regiment. They met with little opposition until they were well into Belgium. In the early evening of May 21st he went on a recce to decide on some movement for the following day. His batman asked: "Do you want me to come with you sir?" "No," said my father, "you just get my kit ready for tomorrow. A private is coming with me" My father and Private Kimmins were killed at the same time. It was thought to be an enemy bomb jettisoned from a plane returning from a raid on London.

My father had left three items of gold behind in England: a cigarette case, a watch and chain (which he wore on a waistcoat) and a little pair of cufflinks. With him in Belgium he had a superb Patek Philippe gold wristwatch. On the 22 May a local farmer came across my dead father. He removed from the obviously dead English officer his pay book, a couple of shopping bills and he also took the Patek Philippe from my father's wrist. The farmer took them home and hid them in a chest of drawers. He decided not to tell his wife – supposedly because she would have been angry with him.

Twenty five years later the farmer died and his wife discovers my father's belongings in her husband's handkerchief drawer. She realized immediately how they came to be there and made the decision to return the items – the watch certainly – to the widow, my mother. This proved to be not at all straightforward. My mother, in the intervening years, had married Colonel Jack Horner and spent time with him in Virginia. When she returned to England and divorced Horner, she married Peter Carlos-Clarke. The War Office eventually discovered that she had divorced Carlos-Clarke and was now living in a flat in Cadogan Gardens in London.

She called me and asked me to lunch with her. "Just you," she said, "Not Pam or the children. I'll explain when I see you." Out of the blue, my mother produced the various items and the accompanying letter which had come from the farmer's wife. Among the possessions there was a bill for £35 for carpet from Peter Jones, the department store in Sloane Square. "I don't think we ever paid that bill for that carpet!" she said. She went on to say:

"Because I gave Michael the gold cigarette case and Johnnie the watch and chain and you just had the cufflinks, I want you to have the Patek watch – which I will have completely over-hauled and cleaned for you." I asked her who had written his initials, G.A.W. on the back of the watch. The watch had been given to him by Stella Nissen (yes, of Nissen hut fame) – a millionairess who had been in love with my father for a long time. "But she always gave me something at the same time," said my mother. "The year she gave him the watch I was given that clock that we generally have on the mantelpiece over the sitting room fire. I think Marks and Spencer used to sell them for about ten pounds." Needless to say this Patek Philippe watch is my most precious possession. I am wearing it today.

I was asked the other day which, out of all the houses I have lived in, stands out as my favourite. It has to be Wickers. We were not there long but it holds an enormous place in my heart. It's a combination of things: the age I was; the house itself – which enveloped us like a well loved garment; the setting – not only where it was in the countryside but the garden itself, created by my father. And, I think, I look back to a particularly golden time of my life, late boyhood. Big school (Eton) just around the corner, and impending manhood; but in the meantime I was a boy in the countryside at just the right age. Other boys might decide that, at age twelve, it might be time to head towards the bright city lights, but I was just so happy to be there. I went back the other day. I stood in the garden (apologies to the lovely owners of Wickers who may have seen a man and a woman of a certain age revolving on their lawn, pointing at things) and smelled the air. There was a very distant hum of traffic but mostly it was the peace and the birdsong and the trees ruffling with an untoward gentleness. They have built a conservatory, which we did not have, but the most astonishing revelation was that the design and layout of the garden is as my father designed it. Although they have closed off the little gate from the road, the brick path he built is still there, meandering in a couple of gentle curves down to the lawn overhung with mature lavenders and other sweet smelling shrubs that brush your legs as you pass. To the left of the path, as you come down it, my father built terraces, because of the slope.

I remembered he commandeered friends who came to visit or stay to move earth, lay bricks and generally muck in. He was persuasive and fun and in garden design, at least, inspirational. And what so impressed me the other day was that his vision still stands. He must have stood on the lawn where I was and seen the woods on the other side of the road rise up the hill and worked out the layers of seamless design, creating a garden that melds so

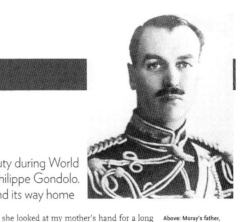

Twenty-five years after his father died on active duty during World War II, Moray Watson finally inherited his Patek Philippe Gondolo. Glyn Brown hears the story of how the watch found its way home

At his book-lined home in southwest London, the acclaimed character actor Moray Watson is showing me a heroic, well-traveled, and immensely cherished Patek Philippe wristwatch that once belonged to his father. It's not unusual, of course, to be given your father's watch, but in this case there's a little more to it; in particular, that it came to Moray 25 years after his father's death.

The watch – an exquisite, slim but sturdy gold art deco-style Gondolo – was given to Gerard Arthur Watson around 1930 by the society millionairess Stella Nissen, who was deeply in love with him. It's not difficult to see what captivated her. In a photograph taken at the start of World War II, Captain Gerard Watson could be a chiseled matinee idol, even in his army uniform.

"I met Stella Nissen," says Moray now. "She lived in Grosvenor House on London's Park Lane and was very elegant and quite friendly to small children. She invited us all to watch George VI's coronation from her bedroom window. And her husband was a great polo player. But she'd absolutely fallen for my father. She gave him a present every year on his birthday. This watch, which has his initials engraved on the back, was given to him when he was still in his twenties."

It's a slight infringement, actually, when Stella knew Gerard was married to the luminous Jean. "Oh, I know!" A chuckle. "Stella would always give my mother a gift at the same time. The year my father had this, she gave my mother a clock from [British chain store] Marks & Spencer."

The Watsons settled with their three young sons in Chelsea, London, where Gerard, a shipbroker, was also a member of the Territorial Army. When war broke out, they moved to Petworth in Sussex, in the southeast of England. "My father wanted his family to be safe. In London, you could hear the bombs coming down in neighboring streets. And I'm very fond of Petworth now, because it's the last place where we were all together."

Gerard joined the 4th Battalion of the Royal Sussex Regiment, and in February 1940, he set off for France. He left behind three of his most prized possessions: a magnificent cigarette case, a pocket watch and chain, and a pair of cufflinks. "But he wore the Patek Philippe watch. He never took that off." Moray pauses. "Just after he'd gone, my mother visited friends for dinner. There was a palm reader there, who told all the other ladies, Oh, this and that will happen... But

she looked at my mother's hand for a long time, then folded her fingers over her palm and said, 'I'm sorry, I'm tired.' I think she'd seen what would happen."

The Royal Sussex arrived in Normandy and marched "more or less non-stop across northern France. They didn't meet any opposition until they got to Belgium." On the night of May 20, Gerard, then the commander of D company, left with one of his men to check the next day's route. "And that was it. Both of them were killed." Gerard was 39. To remember him, Jean gave her eldest son, Michael, the cigarette case, second son, Johnnie, the pocket watch, and the youngest, Moray, then 11, the cufflinks.

Life went on. Jean, a ravishing woman and still very young, eventually remarried and moved first to Virginia, U.S.A., and then back to England. Moray left Eton College and developed a stellar acting career, appearing on stage in London's West End and New York, on TV, and in films opposite the likes of Robert Mitchum, Cary Grant, and Laurence Olivier.

Then in 1965, 25 years after Gerard was killed, Moray's mother called, asking to see him. When he arrived, she produced the Patek Philippe watch, his father's army pay book, and a letter. It transpired that a Belgian farmer had found Gerard's body and taken the watch from his wrist, along with one or two other things – "including a bill from Peter Jones department store, which my mother says we never paid!" The farmer took it all home and hid it in a handkerchief drawer. When he died, his wife found this cache and traced the family through the War Office. Like a faithful hound, the watch had found its way home; now Jean wanted Moray to have it because, long ago, he'd received the smallest memento.

"The astonishing thing is that the watch was in working order, it wasn't touched at all by the bombing," says Moray. "As soon as my mother wound it, it began ticking. And it had been with my father to the very end. In its own way, it's heroic. A miracle." Perhaps also, it's as if Moray has his father's heartbeat with him, ticking, his spirit continuing. He nods. "The watch is so unobtrusive and fits so closely, it's as if it's part of one's body."

Moray plans to leave the watch to his own son, Robin, but for now you feel it's happy where it is, conveying a sense of assurance. "Exactly." Moray smiles. "Just saying, 'I'm here.'"◆

We would like to hear other stories about Patek Philippe watches and their owners for possible publication in the magazine. Please email us at lifeandtimes@patek.com

Above: Moray's father, Captain Gerard Watson, cuts a dashing figure in his army uniform, photographed at the start of World War II. Below: the art deco-style Gondolo given to Gerard around 1930 by the smitten millionairess, Stella Nissen

effortlessly into the woods. Your eye is drawn inexorably upwards – and then down again. Quite, quite beautiful. And moving, very moving. For a brief moment I was twelve again, the woods and their squirrels were out there, Mr Smith was swerving round my legs, Michael and Johnnie were getting their guns and I was holding the dray stick. My father was putting in another series of plants or maybe he was paying attention to his Zinnias – he was passionate about Zinnias and had a fine collection - and my mother – well she was probably with her friend Dee Goody, or with Violet Leconfield. The sense of freedom was immense and for a moment I captured the sense of "all before me".

The cottage itself is charming; mellow pinkish Sussex brick with French and sash windows and an aura of happiness. My bedroom, shared with Johnnie, was on the corner of the house overlooking the garden and my parents were in the room next door – also looking onto the garden. And it seemed to me that the current owners love it as much as we did. The garden is still lovely and obviously they are avid plant lovers. I wish them all the enjoyment we had.

At thirteen and a half I went to Eton. My house master was the estimable CRN (Dick) Routh. He and my father had been at Christchurch College, Oxford together. I suspect that due to my father's death and my mother left penniless, he wangled matters with Eton's bursar and Claude Elliott, the Headmaster, so that my brothers and I were there without paying any fees.

I think that Dick Routh represented the best example of house-mastership. He was caring, knowledgeable, likeable and, looking back, a remarkable psychologist. He was in *loco parentis*, after all, and he did his level best with all of us. I don't think that I was marked out for any special kindnesses; he treated us all in the same way, but I am exceptionally grateful for his being there. He was an example of the modern pastoral care, way before it became the norm. When he retired from Eton, he took a position at Charlecote Park, in Warwickshire – that exquisite example of Elizabethan house, owned by the Fairfax-Lucy's, where he remained until his death.

I was the good boy at Eton. My brother Johnnie was always getting into scrapes. He seemed to have no fear of punishment and was frequently caned. When we were all there together, Michael was Watson Major, Johnnie was Watson Minor and I was Watson Minimus. Of course I moved up to being Minor when Michael left. The only time I was ever caned was after my friend Michael Walker and I were invited by two senior boys to play bridge in the attic of our House. One of our number, who was all gung-ho about the expedition, ratted on us to the powers that be. I was furious. But it was not to be the only time that I had been told that "better was expected of me". I think because I toed the line I was able to see the outcome of stepping off the line, as it were, and I didn't like the consequences; so unlike Johnnie who never cared about the penalties of being caught. He was once caned for being caught in a cinema in Slough. It is probably one of the traits that made him such an excellent army man.

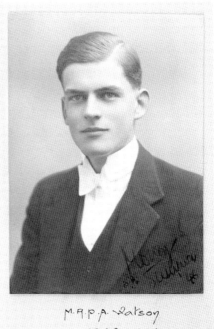

M.A.P.A. Watson
1942-1946.

My mother still took us to the theatre at the beginning and the end of the holidays. It was at a performance of Terence Rattigan's Flare Path that the future of my life was set. This play, written in 1941 and first produced in 1942, was about the separation and tensions that war causes, about loss, love and betrayal. I remember Michael and Johnnie laughing and crying in all the right places. I did too. But my overwhelming memory is of pure immersion in the glamour of the theatre. And by glamour I do not mean a starry glamour, I mean glamour in the witchcraft sense. I was glamorized. I was spellbound. I was mesmerised. It wasn't just the story or the acting: it was the dialogue, the exits and entrances, the set changes. It was the mechanics and the craft and theatre as a whole. And I knew that I wanted to be a part of that. I knew that this was what I wanted to do with my life. Not until later did I realise that this was a strange career to wish to choose.

I must have been about fifteen. My classics master was Oliver John Hunkin, whose father, incidentally, was Bishop of Truro. At the end of class one morning I went up to Mr Hunkin's desk and said "Do you think, sir, it would be possible to do a reading of a play in class one day?" "No, Watson, I'm afraid it would not be possible". "You seem very adamant, Sir." "Yes, I'm afraid I am. I had considered doing exactly what you suggested so I asked the Headmaster about it. He said 'no it's not a good idea for two reasons: (i) it would distract them from their usual work and that would be reflected in their exam results and (ii) it might encourage homosexuality'" "Good heavens, Sir, what's that?" "Boys liking boys." "Well, I'm very fond of Michael

Walker and Ralph Assheton and Michael McCreery." "No, not like that. Liking them....well....too much...." "Oh. I see." But I didn't and I have to say that this notion struck me as a very weird thing indeed.

Anyway that was that and I really didn't know what he was talking about! Indeed the only play that was put on in School Hall during my time was a production of *Henry IV Part 1* directed by John Barton, who was one of my fellow students. He became a professional director and joined the newly formed Royal Shakespeare Company in the early 60s as one of Peter Hall's assistant directors, and eventually became one of the RSC's Associate Directors. He became well-known for his absentmindedness: even going on holiday leaving his kettle boiling in his office at the theatre. Then, as I came to a position of seniority in the school, Dick Routh asked me to be House captain. Me: "But surely there are several people who would be better than me, Jeremy or Michael for instance". Dick: "Well no. That's just the point. They are all going to university and you are going to be an actor. All the empathy that that entails makes you far more suitable to be Captain of the house". So Captain of the house I became. Was I a good one? I have no idea. But I did like the fact that responsibility was given to me on merit.

At the end of the holidays in 1943 my mother took we three boys to see *Something In The Air* with Jack Hulbert and Cicely Courtneidge. They were, between the wars, quite possibly Britain's leading comedy pairing, having appeared in many successful shows in the West End.

Something In The Air was a revue specifically designed to boost morale in the darker days of the war. At the interval the curtains parted slightly and Miss Courtneidge came out and folded them behind her. She spoke eloquently on behalf of the North Sea Fishermen who were having a duff time of it and urged each member of the audience to donate generously. She and the rest of the cast, as well as the usherettes, would be in the foyer afterwards with buckets to accept all generosities. My mother gave us each a sixpence to put in the bucket. I was determined to give my sixpence to no one but Miss Courtneidge and so made a beeline for her after the performance. I was still small enough to get lost among all the adult playgoers and I vanished to all intents and purposes. I found Miss Courtneidge and gave her my sixpence. She gave me such a brilliant smile and thanked me as if my donation had been a hundred times as large. She looked just as marvellous up close as she did on the stage. I thought her wonderful and was basking in her smile when I heard "Oh there you are! We were wondering what had become of you!" My mother quite thought she had lost me. "Well, Mummy, I had to put my sixpence in Miss Courtneidge's bucket."

After the death of my father my mother took up with an American colonel, Jack Horner. Although I didn't care for him much, as did neither of my brothers, I can just about see why she might. I can also see why she would want to. She was a glamorous, beautiful and sexy woman. She enjoyed a social life. Horner was not tall but stocky and muscular. I suspect he exuded sex appeal as well, although even in retrospect I can't see it. But there is no accounting for Eros. He did have a dynamism – often found in that type of physical combination. I also suspect my mother enjoyed sex. Horner pestered her to marry him. She was perfectly happy not being married. Horner was, I think, just a good liaison for her. But he wore her down to the point where she told him that she would marry him if he gave up drinking. She thought herself safe. So it was with considerable surprise that she found herself engaged; Horner gave up drinking the day after she had offered him a reason. She married him and went off to live in Virginia. She didn't tell us *per se*. She discussed it with Michael and when I say 'discuss' it was barely that. It was more a question of "I'm thinking of going to America with Jack Horner – getting married of course. How do you feel?" Michael, who, as I said, did not care for Horner much, responded with something fairly noncommittal such as we were old enough to look after ourselves. So that's what happened. I don't remember any particular feeling of abandonment. I was 14 after all and considered myself way on the road to adulthood. Being at school and away from home since the age of seven does inculcate some kind of resilience, even if it means an emotional distancing. But that was something I was not aware of at the time.

Over the years I have come to realise that there are women and there are mothers. And my mother wasn't a mother. It wasn't that she was selfish, just that she saw no reason why having children should impinge on what she wanted to do with her life. Which is interesting in its own way.

There were downsides and upsides to this event of my mother zipping off to the USA. Downsides: the necessity of having to stay with my aunt Norma in Hare Street, Buntingford, Hertfordshire. After the country joys of Petworth, the ability to endlessly ramble in the woods and over the fields, the move to flat dull Hertfordshire was awful. I liked Aunt Norma, but being plonked down in the middle of, to me, nowhere made my heart sink.

By the time we stayed with Norma, she was no longer married. I don't think she had another relationship with a man. She had produced Jeremy and that was that. When we lived with her in the holidays (Jeremy too, he was at Tonbridge School), she lived with Theodora Tucker who was a dance and movement teacher at various drama schools, including the Webber-Douglas, where I eventually trained.

Before she married, Norma had made a name for herself as a golfer. In 1923/24 she captained the Sheringham Golf Club Ladies team. Her great friend in those days was the legendary Joyce Wethered who won five successive English titles and four of the six British Championships in which she competed. Bobby Jones was her idol and Percy Allis, father of the inimitable Peter, said that if she had been a man she would have been a second Harry Vardon. Aunt Norma loved telling the story of Joyce at the 17th hole at Sheringham on 12th June 1912. There was a big crowd for this particular event and Norma was there in the gallery. The 17th hole runs parallel with the curving coastal railway line which runs from Norwich to Sheringham. On this particular Wednesday in June there was a fast and noisy steam train (I know all trains were steam then but it is still worth mentioning) just coming into sight towards Sheringham. All those who were watching were under the (obvious) assumption that Joyce would either play her shot there and then, or wait until the monster had passed on its way to Sheringham station. But she seemed, to all those onlookers, to wait for the exact moment when this large noisy train was as close as it could possibly be before she struck the ball. The strike was successful. It went where Joyce intended it to go, into the 17th hole. Afterwards Norma asked her why she had not waited for the train to pass by before taking the shot. "What train?" came the answer. The 17th hole at Sheringham is still known as the "What Train?" hole. Incidentally, and nothing to do with golf, Joyce married and became Lady Heathcote-Amory.

Upsides to my mother going away? My housemaster, the remarkable Dick Routh, must have had a quiet word with the parents of all my best friends; the result of which was that every holiday I spent time with them, generally at least a week.

One of those holidays entailed stalking in Scotland. Julian Williams' father had the Strathvaich Estate, halfway between Inverness and Ullapool. I would go up on the sleeper train to Inverness, sometimes with Dick who was often invited. I loved the smell of the compartment, slightly sooty with an aftertaste of impending adventure. There is an astonishing pleasure in lying in that narrow banquette, being rocked by the diddly-dah of the wheels crossing the joins of the rails. In the Inverness morning we would take another train to Garve where we would be met and driven to Strathvaich.

After breakfast we would be assigned a ghillie and head off for the moors. I always thought it magic the way the ghillie would know where the deer were at any given time. We would walk for a while, that steady short stepped stride necessary for making way over heather and tuft and rock and boggy ground. Make your stride even, steady and short and you cover a remarkable distance. So we would walk in the direction suggested by the ghillie and after some time, always a variable time, we would sight the deer about half a mile away. From then it was down on your belly folks and curve round to keep them upwind of us. There is a certain smell of Scottish moorland, bog myrtle and heather, sheep droppings and peat. It is a combination like no other. And crawling on our stomachs slowly over the landscape puts it in your nose. We would crawl for ages like this until, putting our heads slowly above the parapet of a low ridge; there would be the stag about 30 yards ahead. I learnt how to gralloch a stag. I had a pair of antlers for ages. I remember them at Aunt Norma's but they got lost somewhere along the road of life.

Dick Routh must also have asked my close friend at Eton, Michael Walker, if I could stay with him in Rutland. Michael's father commuted every day to Leicester, where he was Chairman of Wolsey socks. His mother, Dickie (his brother) and his sister, Boo, and I would go hunting with the Cottesmore hounds. Yes, I was unlucky to lose my father in Belgium and my mother to an American Colonel in Virginia, but lucky to have such good friends at school.

As well as stalking in Scotland and hunting in the Shires, I also stayed with Jeremy Fisher and his family who lived at Offham, near Lewes in Sussex. Jeremy's father was chairman of Barclays Bank and his mother and sister sang at the Albert Hall in the Bach Choir. Jeremy was eventually to be my best man when I married Pam in Chelsea Old Church in 1955.

Then, straight out of Eton, I went into the army.

3
Oh – the Life of a Soldier…

In 1946, immediately after leaving Eton I was called up for National Service. Conscription was from 18 onwards. I was sent to Colchester barracks. I remember little about my time there except that it consisted of square-bashing, of learning how high to raise one's arms when marching and how to properly salute an officer. All useful stuff, obviously. We were confined to barracks for the first month. This was, I think, to prevent the men absconding. For anyone who had been to boarding school it wasn't a problem – just an extension of what had been most of one's life for the previous 10 or so years. But for others, straight from family life and without the "benefit" of having left one's parents ages ago, it was a rude shock. Many were desperately unhappy and homesick and might have run away if not confined. For me, all these 27 lads were an education. I had only mixed with my own background until now and being among what was to me an almost alien species was an education. They rapidly became less alien and more down to earth, real and a lot of fun. In fact we all became mates quite quickly.

On my first day out I found the local theatre and saw a play. No idea what it was but it was an interlude, back to my own intended world, for a time. I returned to Colchester's Meanee Barracks somewhat later than I should have but just in time nevertheless. All of the lads were in there. All 27 of them. As I walked in, one of my mates, sitting at the far end of the barrack room saw me come in and shouted: "Well done, Moray – good to 'ave yer back. 'Ad a bit of cunt 'ave yer?". My reply, whatever it was (and honestly I didn't really know what to say) was drowned, thank heavens, by the laughter.

I was interviewed to find out which regiment I would like to join. I gave the Royal Sussex as first choice, because of my father obviously, the Norfolk as my second choice because my mother came from that county, and the 60th Rifles, because it was my brother Michael's regiment. I was determined to become an officer. Not because I wanted to be posh or necessarily be in command, but because I just did not want to be yelled at by CSMs and RSMs. There was quite enough of that in the training to last a lifetime and was probably a contributory cause of my deafness, all that shouting in my ear. So I applied for the WOSB (War Office Selection Board). I passed but had to endure many weeks at the 28th Training Battalion at the Hollywood Barracks about a mile east of Belfast. The endurance was made harder by the worst winter in years, even for Belfast.

I had been training for 28 weeks, over half a year, when I was marched down to the Adjutant's office. The adjutant turned out to be an aggressive member of the Royal Ulster Rifles. To this day I cannot bear the Northern Irish accent and it is all because of him. I had no idea what was coming. The exchange went like this: Adjutant: "Watson! Have you been writing to the War Office?" Me: "No Sir." Adjutant: "Is there a particular reason why you should go to the United States of America?" Me: "Perhaps, sir, because my mother has married an American army colonel and is living with him in Virginia." Adjutant: "I'll look into this further. Return to your platoon."

A week later: Adjutant: "Now. Watson. It seems that, via his ADC, Field Marshall Sir Henry Maitland Wilson has requested for you to visit your mother for two weeks." (Pause). "You do realise that, if you do so, when you return to the 28th Training Battalion you will be relegated to the first week of training?" Me: "Yes Sir." Adjutant: "Dismiss."

I thought going to Virginia was worth the risk of having to start again in the first week of training because somehow I just thought it would not happen. Oh the optimism of an eighteen year old.

All the above came about because my mother had become a good friend of Hester Wilson, the wife of Sir Henry "Jumbo" Wilson. (Jumbo because he was a big man.) Together my mother and Hester decided to tackle Jumbo about Johnnie and me coming to visit for a week or two. Hester, incidentally, unlike all their other intimates, did not call her husband Jumbo; she called him "Tweet Tweet". My mother asked her why she did this? "Well," said Hester "Don't *you* think he looks just like a bird looking out of a nest?" And it was via Hester, therefore, and thence to Jumbo and thence to Jumbo's ADC, Major John Miller DSO MC, a Welsh Guards Officer, that my visit to the US was arranged. I can see now why the Adjutant in Belfast didn't like the idea: I was getting above my station.

Major Miller looked and sounded like a typical chinless wonder, a proper caricature of a Guards officer, with a stoop and a limp hand-shake, easily dismissed as a nincompoop – think Captain Darling in Blackadder. That, however, would be a mistake, a mistake that the Americans made. They thought that the DSO and MC were just routine awards for being in the army, long service medals or suchlike. They were not aware that they were gallantry medals for bravery in the face of extreme danger. They continued to dismiss him until they saw him on the hunting field, mounting a different horse each meet (not many people can do that successfully) and jumping the most fearsome obstacles when hounds were running, obstacles that few of them would dream of taking on with any degree of equanimity let alone ability. Then they changed their minds.

I liked Major John Miller. After leaving the Army, Lt-Colonel John Miller became Crown Equerry in charge of the Royal Mews and all attendant equestrian and ceremonial affairs. He was knighted in 1974.

So to Virginia we went. Johnnie had just finished his cadetship at Eaton Hall in Cheshire and was then at Sandhurst. He was on the road to becoming a professional soldier and an officer. Sandhurst was still on a war footing as hostilities had only ended eighteen months earlier and there was still a massive job for the army to do. Things did not just stop on VE day. It was a good time to make a career of the army.   Johnnie had the right temperament to make a success of it. Johnnie (The Officer) and I (The Rifleman in the 60th Rifles) boarded the *Samaria* in Liverpool. The *Samaria* was full of Canadian soldiers who were going back home after being demobbed. There are three things I remember about that voyage. The first was that officers and men were not allowed to mix. Segregation is all in spite of our being brothers, so if we were to meet, it had to be surreptitious. I remember finding my way to one of the funnels and being obliged to give Johnnie some of my issue of the famous American Hershey Bar chocolate which had been given to the soldiers, but not to the officers. My first taste of chocolate for about seven years. I did not exactly enjoy sharing it!

The second thing I remember was being required to strip naked and present ourselves to four seated medical officers, hold our hands up high, then turn about and bend over. That way the medics were supposed to discover if any of us had contracted any diseases from any young German ladies, or indeed any ladies, in Europe. It made no difference to them that I had not been out of England. Protest as I might, I was a soldier and a private and among troops so obviously my privates were to be "examined". I had to go along with it. I remember a feeling of deep humiliation standing stark naked before these seated strangers. My cheeks go pink even now at the thought.

The third memory is that it seemed to me that the Samaria was going excessively fast through a very heavy sea. The ship was rising on huge waves and we were slamming bow down in the troughs. I asked the purser about it. He confirmed it was as I thought . The captain was driving too fast but "he had his orders" to get the Canadian troops, every single last soldier of the 1000 on board, back home for Christmas and the purser said "we should have left Liverpool earlier…" Of course it was not just a question of making landfall in Canada in time for Christmas as the men then had to get back to wherever their homes were, and that could have been 4000 miles the other side of the north American continent. So the Captain was under pressure.

We docked in Halifax, Nova Scotia, on 18 December. Johnnie and I took a train to Montreal and thence to Washington DC. We had a great reunion with Mama, of course. We had not seen her for four or five years. She and Jack Horner lived in a house called Mells Paddock, adjoining the stables of the Old Dominion Hunt in northern Virginia. Jack was the joint master of the Old Dominion. So naturally we went hunting. My hunting experience had been with the Cottesmore in Rutland so that stood me in good stead – long fast runs over particularly large cut and laid hedges – and I was able to enjoy the Old Dominion. There was quite some similarity between the countryside of Virginia and the Cottesmore country so one could be deceived and lulled into thinking that you knew what you were going to be facing. But the fields seemed to be twice the size and the fences were huge zig-zag rails. You had to turn your horse through ninety degrees in order to jump them. I do remember Jumbo Wilson coming out with us even though it was difficult to find a horse for him as he was around 18 stone.

Johnnie came down with jaundice while we were there and spent a few days in the Walter Reed hospital in Washington. The doctors prescribed a month's leave for him. Jack told me that as jaundice was contagious I could stay on as long as Johnnie. But I liked Horner no better than before, although he was perfectly affable, and I said that in reality I should get back to my barracks in Ireland. I was also mindful of the Adjutant's threats of relegating me to the beginning of training.

So I returned to the 28th Training Battalion abroad the *Aquitania*, a vast four funnelled ship. I had only been on board one day when I realised that I was being followed by a man. He was quite short, thickset and had a predatory and lecherous smile which he flashed at every turn. It was obvious that he was after my body. I was, quite frankly, terrified. I thought I would be safe in the cinema when a showing of a film was announced. But foolishly, instead of sitting down in the stalls right opposite the screen and in full view of everyone behind, I thought I would be safer in the dress circle. Mistake. I wasn't. He sought me out and I ran for my life. I think I spent the remainder of the voyage in my cabin. Looking back, it is interesting that, in spite of being 19 and to most intents and purposes an adult, there were serious gaps in my knowledge. Boarding school makes you adult beyond your years in terms of emotional self-sufficiency but there are things in the big wide world that it cannot prepare you for and after that close encounter I knew it. It is the same naivety as not knowing what a homosexual was at school. I remember I felt as frightened as someone ten years younger might have been.

Back in England, or rather Northern Ireland, the bastard adjutant carried out his threat to take me back to first base again in the training. But, that done, I passed on to Eaton Hall in Cheshire. I was reasonably happy there and actually managed to complete my time properly without being dragged back to the beginning again. I met Jeremy Morse there and we were friends for a time although we did not retain the friendship. I pursued my career as an actor while he became a hugely successful banker, Chairman of Lloyds and Chancellor of the University of Bristol. Years later I was doing my one man show called *Ancestral Voices* in a building immediately behind the Ritz Hotel in Piccadilly. Lady Morse was in charge of the event. She invited me and my boss, Hugh Massingberd, to attend their final meeting to decide where I should dress and perform. When I came to say goodbye I said "By the way, Lady Morse, I was in the army with your husband." "Oh were you," she said, "and where were you both stationed?"

"Well, we were at OCTU together and, of course, I remember Jeremy because he got the Sword of Honour" "He did indeed. And, Mr Watson, does your memory serve you well enough to remember that, after receiving the Sword of Honour, he marched the entire battalion off in the wrong direction!"

"No," I said, "my memory does not serve me that well."

"Well – I sometimes remind him!"

I don't remember for the simple reason that I was in that battalion that was being marched off. We went where we were told and if we were about turned in the wrong direction how were we to know? Seemed all right to us and orders is orders….

Spittal, Austria 1947/48

I was commissioned into the Essex Regiment. There was no room for me in my three choices of regiment, the Royal Sussex, Norfolk and 60th Rifles. However, there were orders at the time for all new subalterns to be sent abroad if possible. Because of this I was drafted into the Northamptonshire Regiment which had just spent months in Berlin, followed by a spell in Trieste but was now in Spittal in Eastern Austria. This was a very easy posting, chosen for the Northamptonshires I think, because the Berlin tour had been very demanding and they deserved a softer life for a while.

We had been there a week when we received a visit from General Galloway. He asked to speak to all the officers. "Expect you are wondering why you are here. Well, I'll tell you. There are, as you may know, four regiments in Austria: The Scots Guards, a Yorkshire regiment, the Ox and Bucks Light Infantry and you. Now, Marshal Tito, President of Yugoslavia, knows you are all here so he won't invade. If he changes his mind he will come over the border with planes, tanks and God knows what else. YOU WILL BE WIPED OUT." A silence followed by reserved and nervous laughter. Just like *Beyond the Fringe*: "Perkins." "Sir?" "We need a futile gesture at this stage. Take a plane and fly into France." "Sir." "And Perkins?" "Sir?" "Don't come back." "Yes sir. Sir? Is it au revoir?" "No Perkins. Goodbye". Same sort of thing.

I was in Spittal with an old school friend, Henry Pickthorn. We had both successfully passed out of OCTU, but I suspect he was as equally unsuited for a life in uniform as I. Together we decided to attend German classes with an old lady who lived in the village, but we had not been there above three weeks when I was sent on a cross country exercise. We were dressed entirely in white – just like the Heroes of Telemark or any of the James Bond films where there is a ski chase. We walked miles and we skied miles. In fact I really enjoyed it. The crispness of both air and snow and the freedom and fun of being outdoors again doing something sporty. Years later, when I was telling someone about this, they remarked that it was just as well the lessons had been cut short because the German I would have learned from a lady in Spittal would never have been understood in Hamburg or Munich.…

One day after returning to Spittal I reported to the company commander, Ted Kitchen, who told me to report to the Adjutant. My immediate thought was "Oh Lord. What have I done now?" I was not the most brilliant of 2nd lieutenants. I faced the Adjutant: stout, pompous and humourless. Think Captain Mainwaring in *Dad's Army* and you have him.

Adjutant: "Ah, Watson. Come in. Sit down. Good news for you, good news for the Regiment. You have been selected to be ADC to General Galloway. What about that?"

Me: "Wonderful Sir. I'm very flattered. When would I begin?"

Adjutant: "It seems to be within the next 2 or 3 weeks. All right?

Me: "Yes, of course, sir, as long as I can go out with my group, 76C"

Adjutant: "76C? What's that?"

Me: "Well, sir, as you know I am only a temporary soldier"

Adjutant: "When do you expect this 76C to come into effect?"

"Early in September, I hope, sir."

"But that's only…" he counts on his fingers, "one, two, three, 4 ½ months away. The General would expect you to be with him for at least 6 months, possibly nine."

"Oh dear, sir. What a pity."

"Pity? PITY???" Steam out of ears came to mind and like Captain Mainwaring he looked as though the top of his head would explode. "And when you leave the Regiment and become an ordinary citizen, what do you intend to do?"

"Well, sir, I am hoping to become an actor."

"AN ACTOR…" He was horrified. I might just have well said that it had been my burning ambition all my life to become a refuse collector.

So I did not become ADC to General Galloway and, more insultingly, the job went to a young subaltern in the Ox and Bucks Light Infantry. I never asked how the Northamptonshires felt about my refusal….And the adjutant never spoke to me again.

By happy chance, around the same time I was demobbed, my mother had divorced Jack Horner and returned to England. She had "escaped" with the connivance of Al Hinckley, Horner's Joint-Master of the Old Dominion Hunt. Jack had proved to be a jealous husband questioning where she was going, where she had been and who with. He may well have been right – as I have said she was a very attractive woman. And she confided in Al. It took several weeks of poring over timetables and finding tickets but he found her a place on a ship returning to England. She packed in secret and when the day came she upped and left. Al agreed to be at Mells Paddock to meet Jack when he came home, a task that I don't suppose he wanted to do, but for which I applaud him. Later Jack said that he knew he had been somewhat "stifling" but he was so afraid of losing her. And she had become so very bored with being left alone all day while Jack was in Washington. It was a lesson in allowing your loved ones to fly free.

4

Drama School – then into the World

Webber Douglas

Back in London I shared a flat at the top of a house in Roland Gardens with my mother and my brother Michael who was beginning to carve a place for himself in the drinks and brewery trade with Ind Coope & Allsop. Living in Roland Gardens was perfect for me – it was just round the corner from the Webber D.

I had had an interview with W. Johnstone-Douglas, one of the founders of the Webber Douglas School of Drama. The Webber D, as it was known, became my spiritual home. My aunt Norma's (she of Hare Street and my holidays from Eton) friend, Theo Tucker (Theo short for Theodora), the dance teacher, suggested I audition for a place there. Theo taught at all the major drama academies in London including RADA, LAMDA, the Central and Rose Bruford but she considered the Webber D to be the best at the time. RADA in particular was mostly regarded as a finishing school for young ladies rather than a place to turn out any serious actors, although it rose to a position of pre-eminence in the sixties and seventies.

Both Webber & Douglas were distinguished singers. JD was famous for his performance in *The Immortal Hour*, an opera by English composer Rutland Boughton, first performed in 1914 and revived only just recently at the Finborough Theatre. I never met Webber - he must have died before I went there. JD taught singing and diction. There are two other teachers that I remember: Doris Johnstone and Ellen O'Malley. Miss Johnstone took the arriving students in a class which was referred to as Junior Shakespeare. She did not dwell on characterisation but on exits and entrances. This may seem an oblique way of approaching Shakespeare but what she concentrated on was our ability to get into character in the wings; how to effect the change from ordinary mortal to Melancholy Jacques or Puck or Hamlet. Miss J had a permanent cigarette hanging from the middle of her lips. Ellen O'Malley was very distinguished-looking, very elderly (at least from our point of view) and taught the leaving students. She was a great proponent of the works of George Bernard Shaw so that by the time we left we had a good grounding in *Candida, Man and Superman* and in particular *Heartbreak House* because she had been the very first Ellie in that play.

As well as Dancing and Diction (very Alice in Wonderland), we had classes in Movement, Deportment and Fencing. It does all sound like a chapter from Lewis Carroll. Don't get me wrong, it was an enlivening time and we actually learnt a lot about our craft but in the light of the modern day it all sounds a bit archaic. We did have fun, though, even if, occasionally, the fun had consequences. We used to try and get cheap tickets for the theatre. The Webber D was in South Kensington and often we could get tickets for the Lyric Hammersmith. One night at the Lyric we nipped out in the interval and bought fish and chips and took it back inside the auditorium to eat it. Yes. I know. Not really the thing to do, especially not then. All theatre-goers in those days were brought up with the necessity of sitting still and (apart from smoking which everyone did without question) not annoying the fellow members of the audience. Well, in this instance members of the public did complain because of the smell which was a mite stronger than the smell of cigarette. The manager found out who the culprits were and reported it to JD. He called us all into the office and gave us a rocket. He then said to me: "I'm surpassed and particularly shocked by you, Moray". He may have been right but I was furious, I remember, at being singled out like this. Funny how that still sticks with me.

In our final two terms our performances in the little Chanticleer Theatre, part of the Webber D, was opened to the general public, including, we hoped, agents, casting directors and theatre management all in the hope and expectation of future work. Theatre was our aim. Television was not yet there as a medium of professional expression and was not considered by us in any way at all. Film was seen as a lesser art form, suitable only for those who had no talent for the stage. Theatre, in particular West End theatre, was where we wanted to be.

I was spotted by an actor called Salvin Stewart who was forming a company with his father-in-law, Alexander Field. Field had been in the original production of *Journey's End*, by RC Sherriff with Laurence Olivier so there was a bit of gloss and glamour attached to him. The company was to be in Nottingham for six weeks, then on to Whitley Bay, north of Newcastle.

Salvin was to be the leading man; I was to be the juvenile lead. I was thrilled. I was about to embark on the life I had dreamed of for nearly ten years. It is difficult to convey quite how momentous this was in these days of instant fame via the various media that are now available to one and all. Consider what it was like back then when there was at least one theatre in almost every town in the country, delivering a new play a week (or every other week or every three weeks depending on area) to the local audiences; when communication was essentially by letter or telegram or, if you were very lucky, a phone call; when there was no television to prevent an evening audience from venturing out to a place where they could lose themselves for a couple of hours, where they could be involved in a slice of comedy, or a hefty dish of tragedy. This was the world I was entering. I was to be a part of this make-believe, this habitation of character, of delivering feelings and emotion to the audience, in effect a collaborative experience. I was to enjoy the ultimate pleasure of being believed when I stood onstage, of feeling that umbilical communication between actor and audience. The joy of embarking on this journey was overwhelming. I felt lucky, happy - and vindicated. I think that this feeling of joy even superseded the difficulty of separation from Pam Marmont, my future wife.

We had met at the Webber D and had got involved towards the end of our time there. Pam was from a theatrical family. She had landed a part in *Oklahoma* the new musical, playing 'giggling-Gertie' and understudying Ado Annie at Drury Lane in the West End. It was obvious that our meetings would be few and far between, but we were doing what we wanted to do with our lives, regardless of our love for each other.

So off to Nottingham.

Weekly Rep 1950-1952
I am an ACTOR. I am paid. This is real now, and no fantasy. Real to the point of rehearsing and playing from 10 in the morning 'til 10 at night, six days a week. I think we were a happy bunch of people. We started in Nottingham, a new repertory company, a play a week. We did anything from Ben Travers farces to – I was going to say high tragedy but I don't think tragedy was terrifically popular. Most people wanted to be taken out of themselves and although tragedies are cathartic, it is a comedy that tends to put bums on seats. Buthat I was doing what I wanted to do. I had a steady job. I was happy. If there were tensions in the company I was not yet aware of them. In fact I hardly ever was aware of problems – most of it went straight over my head. Don't get me wrong – it's not that I was dumb or anything, but the way I was brought up was to mind my own business and things like emotions and difficulties were frowned on. You just got on with whatever was in front of you, an agreeable chap just getting on with people. And things.

We did 16 plays in 16 weeks. Salvin of course had the plum leads; I played the goofy juvenile, or occasionally got made up as a brigadier, like the one I was to eventually play in *Darling Buds of May*. There was only one time I was on stage alone and that was when we did a revue instead of a play. I think we were intended to tour from Nottingham to Whitley Bay via somewhere or other, possibly Guildford, but it didn't happen so we put on a revue. All I remember is a tight spot on my face, and I sang "If those lips would only speak, if those eyes could only see, but it's only a beautiful picture in a beautiful golden frame". Shades of Browning's *My Last Duchess* I always thought.

We were a close knit company – the stage management was part of the family. Dickinson was the stage manager and also played parts – as did the scenic designer. We all mucked in. Our 16 weeks of rep included Ben Travers' farces *Rookery Nook* and *Marry the Girl*, Frank Vosper's thriller *Love From A Stranger,* and the comedy *The Dover Road* by AA Milne. The farces were mostly Aldwych farces; made popular by the three farceurs, Tom Walls, Ralph Lynn and Robertson Hare (anyone remember *All Gas and Gaiters?*) whose catchphrase was "oh calamity" whenever he lost his trousers which was <u>always</u>.

Ralph Lynn became an overnight success at the age of 40 when, having slogged his guts out in silly ass roles for 20 years, he was cast as the lead in Will Evans' and Arthur Valentine's *Tons of Money*. On the strength of its success, Tom Walls, the co-producer, took up a lease on the Aldwych theatre and spent a successful decade producing the 12 Aldwych farces. I loved the farces. The silly comedy of farce – so typically British and known as low comedy – understated, yet over the top and with excellent wordplay appealed to me – and I had the timing for it. Years later I met Salvin in a film studio in Bristol – I was working on a TV serial but I do not remember what he was doing there – and he said to me: "We used to put the farces on for you, Moray".

By great contrast, *Love From A Stranger* is a psychological thriller. It was highly praised when originally produced in the 30s and we were pretty successful with it in the 50s, but I wonder whether it would be as successful these days although the subject matter, that of a woman marrying in haste to find her husband is not what he seems to be, might resonate with today's romances and affairs conducted over the internet and the infinite ability afforded by that medium to be someone else. Although I do have all the programmes for all the plays we did, the only other play I remember doing at Nottingham is *The Wind And The Rain* by Merton Hodge. This was a joy to do – but I remember nothing of it: I only remember that I enjoyed doing it. It was quite a successful play, running for a couple of years in London and six months on Broadway as well as being translated into nine or so languages. I also have a cutting of the Repertory Roundabout by "Script" from January 1951. Our company is mentioned with praise, including me – my first review. Fame at last. Don't forget – this is the era before television and the stage was still considered the apogee of the acting profession.

Weekly rep was but a stepping stone on the way to the West End where, as happened to Ralph Lynn, one could become an overnight sensation; the new "young" thing, the toast and darling of the theatre-going public and, just the same as it is today, liberally written about in all the gossip papers. Although, of course, one wanted to be written about for one's marvellous ability on the stage rather than for one's infamous capabilities off stage. Nottingham came to an end and we all trooped off to the Priory Theatre in Whitly Bay on the coast east of Newcastle upon Tyne where we were performing over the winter. It must have been cold, what with the wind coming straight at us off the Ural Mountains of Russia but I don't remember whether it was or not.

I do remember that Salvin's wife, Joanna Field, the daughter of company owner Alexander Field, suddenly - just not being there. And it wasn't until I went through my scrap book of cuttings and play leaflets that I realised she must have been away having a baby. Her last play was *Candida* (GBS) in the first week of October 1951; she would have been in her fifth month and so unable to continue on stage. There were no parts for pregnant ladies. If there were parts for an expectant mother it would have been played by a cushion rather than a real live mother to be. Joanna Field gave birth to a daughter on 22 February, 1952. Sometime later she and Salvin were divorced. Salvin married another actress in the company, Joyce Fenby. It transpires that they were having an affair of some quite long standing. I was totally unaware of this. You might think that living and working together I should have picked up the signs but don't forget I was pretty unversed in the ways of the world – even after two years in both the army and at drama school and now, almost, a year in rep. Some kinds of worldly wise matters take a lot of time to understand for someone who was late in becoming streetwise. I had no idea there was anything going on: they lived in another side of the house and I hardly ever came into contact with them. It was not for me to witness the potentially farcical situation of the bedroom swap. I do remember thinking, however, that it was rather sad. I liked

Joanna and thought her a fine actress, much better than Joyce. I've sometimes wondered whether Salvin preferred less opposition from a less talented wife.

Amongst all this intrigue we had plays to learn and perform: *Duet for Two Hands* by Mary Hayley Bell, wife of John Mills and mother of Hayley who starred in the film *Whistle Down the Wind* from a play by MHB; *Love in Albania* by Eric Linklater, which I recall enjoying; *September Tide* by Daphne du Maurier about a 'middle-aged' woman whose son-¬in-law falls for her; and an adaptation of *Vanity Fair*.

Mid-April 1952 saw the end of the Field Company in Whitley Bay. Looking at a cutting of the time it seems that they had been pursuing the possibility of taking up permanent residence in the town but for whatever reason it was not to be. So I was let loose on the world. It was not long, though, before I got another job – this time at the Pendragon Theatre in Reading. Then to Brighton for *The Heiress* by the Goetz husband and wife playwright team – an adaptation of Henry James' *Washington Square* – a tale of a subdued daughter, irascible father and penniless and probably rather unlikeable suitor. It all ends badly with no-one reconciling themselves with each other. Typical James, somewhat repressed, never saying what you mean and only alluding to truth in epigrams. Pretty much the way I was brought up, so it seemed quite normal at the time but, looking back, it does seem very uptight.

All this time I had been without an agent and indeed had not needed one. But now I felt the need and went to see Frazer and Dunlop, then at 25 Wardour Street, Soho. Soho was then a wonderfully seedy place yet full of magic, Italian coffee bars and theatrical agents. I filled out this enormous questionnaire about my capabilities and possibilities and left it with them. A little while later I got a call:

Mr Fraser: "Och Moray – I've got ye a job"
Me: "Oh"
"It's a film: *Where's Charlie?..*"
"Oh"
"It's a musical"
"Musical? Mr Fraser – I can't do that."
"Why on earth not?"
"Well – I can't sing, I can't dance"
"But you ticked them off on the questionnaire"
"Yes, well I ticked riding a motorbike and swimming underwater but I can't

do those either." "But can you dance anything?"
"I can waltz and quickstep"
"And sing? Do you know any songs?"
"Yes. The moment I saw you, I swear that time stood still."
"Right. Sing that."
Me singing: "The moment I saw you, I swear that time stood still…"
"NOT NOW. Sing that at the audition."

So I do. I sing and I dance and then I am handed a rugby ball and asked if I knew what it was. Yes. Of course I did. We start throwing the ball around. That was something that I could do. I had played rugby at Allen House. Then came: "Well, we'll let you know". Words, I must admit, that I have heard far too often in my life. It is a refrain that an actor must become accustomed to and you never really get over it. It induces a small drop in the stomach and that tinge of despair that flavours the journey home. I went home feeling pretty unhappy. A few days later I get a call. It's Jimmy Fraser. "They want you, Moray." "Who wants me?" "*Where's Charlie?* of course". Well blow me down. "What they said", continued Fraser, "was that your singing was good, your dancing adequate and your football skills were excellent." *Where's Charlie?*, directed by David Butler was loosely based on *Charlie's Aunt*, the play by Brandon Thomas. The music and lyrics were by Frank Loesser and the book by George Abbot. *Where's Charley?* had started on Broadway in 1948 with Ray Bolger in the leading role; he won a Tony for the Best Performance by a Leading Actor in a Musical for his portrayal of Jack Chesney, an Oxford undergraduate about to leave university.

It is another pretty silly farce, semi-pantomime, involving men dressing as women to fool other men and is full of languishing love, strict guardians and pretty girls. It also contains that famous line, said by Donna Lucia that she comes from Brazil "where the nuts come from". There are a couple of songs which were incredibly well known at the time – *Always in love with Amy* sung by Ray and *My Darling, My Darling*. Both of them have long since dropped into the receptacle entitled Songs Which Were Once Famous But No-one Knows Them Anymore.

All in all it was perfect fare for the cinema going audience at the time. And there was I, twenty-two, in my first film and thinking how ludicrous it was for a man in his 60s to be playing an undergraduate. Of course, Ray wasn't in his 60s – he was 48. But to a callow youth anyone over forty is just simply too old for anything. It isn't until you reach the dizzier ages (such as mine) that you learn the differentiation. Now it works the other way round – anyone under 65 is a mere stripling.

Just to temporarily digress, and on the subject of singing, one of the very few times that I have sung on stage came about, as so much does in life, in a rather roundabout way. Years after doing *Where's Charley*, Brian Rix asked me to step into his shoes in *Two Into One* at the Garrick Theatre while he and his wife took a two week holiday in Cornwall. I was to take over the other leading part as soon as he returned to London. My old school friend, Nigel Leigh-Pemberton (who now called himself Nigel Douglas) was playing round the corner in the Coliseum in *The Merry Widow*. He was living in Kent and I was in West Sussex. By happy chance, one night, we found ourselves walking together across Trafalgar Square towards Charing Cross Station to catch our train home. About three months later Nigel called me to ask if I might be interested in taking part in an operetta he was co-directing called *The Gypsy Princess* at Sadler's Wells Theatre. It was a good part – much longer than the average operetta – and it coincided with the ending of *Two Into One*. So I read the script and told Nigel that I would love to do it. And I did! It was a wonderful production and I was thrilled to take part.

Anyway, back to the story. After *Where's Charley* I joined the Mobile Theatre Company which did, as they say, exactly what it says on the side of the van. We were mobile and we were a theatre company and mobile to the extent that we played only one night in each venue. We were touring *Black Chiffon*, in which Dame (although she was not Dame then) Flora Robson had secured a hit at the Westminster Theatre. Flora had the capacity to make you feel as though you were the one person she had been waiting to talk to all day; genuinely warm and a good friend.

Sheila Peers, who was in my year at the Webber-Douglas, was also in the company. Her father, Donald Peers, was a singer who was known during the 1940s for *In A Shady Nook by a Babbling Brook* and later became a pop star, or the 50's equivalent, with songs such as *A Slow Boat to China*. In the early 60s he had his own TV programme *Donald Peers Presents* in which he introduced Tom Jones to the world.

With the Mobile Theatre we crisscrossed England, arriving at our destination in the morning, setting up during the afternoon, playing in the evening and then striking and packing and on to the next destination. I don't remember how I travelled or where I stayed but I do remember that it was exciting, unpredictable, and tiring: and yet we did feel as if we were doing some good even if that does seem a somewhat pious and condescending sentiment. Certainly it seemed that we were appreciated. However, when it was offered, I was not unhappy to accept a position on the HM Tennant stage management team for *The Mortimer Touch*, another play by the prolific Eric Linklater. It was adapted from Ben Jonson's *The Alchemist* into a comedy starring Roger Livesey as Professor Mortimer, Linklater's equivalent of Jonson's Subtle. Pamela Brown played Connie O'Leary who corresponded to Doll Common.

The production opened at the Duke of York's Theatre on 30 April 1952 – the premiere had been at the Edinburgh Festival in 1950. There are three things I remember about *The Mortimer Touch*: during understudy runs Harold Arneil, the stage director and one of the old school, always asked me to stand in for him because he had to do the wages; that Livesey had spoilt his voice in rep and had a rather odd delivery; and that one evening, while I was delivering the Personal Props (those props needed just before going on stage) Livesey said to me: "Do you take personal props to Miss Brown?" I said that I did. "Do you talk to her?" I said "only a little". "I have no conversation at all with her" he said, "At all." And yet here they were playing opposite each other, supposedly sparking off each other on stage and yet with no connection between the two, at least as far as Livesey was concerned. Where the fault lay I do not know. Pamela was like a pussy cat, feline, fey, elegant; he was very hetero and down to earth and, although he had starred in many films, he was not your archetypal leading man. If ever chalk and cheese met – it was here.

My next job was as an actor at the Royal Court Theatre in Sloane Square, just newly refurbished and, according to The Times: "elegantly intimate in crimson and gold". The Court had been bombed right at the beginning of the war so had been derelict for nigh on twelve years and they reopened with *The Bride of Denmark Hill* by two American dramatists, Lawrence Williams and Nell O'Day. This is a play about John Ruskin (played in this production by Andrew Osborn) and the breakup of his non-consummated marriage to Effie Gray (Barbara Murray) who eventually went off with John Everett Millais (Clement McCallin). The Spectator's Gerard Fay described it in a pretty lukewarm and short review as "A fair reopening only for one of our most historic modern theatres"; but I received two reviews (one from the great JC Trewin) with praise for my one line: "No – there's no reply to that piece of paper." So I was happy!

Then back to Brighton before a transfer to the Lyric Hammersmith with *The Gladiators* – which became *The Square Ring* – by Ralph Peterson, a New Zealander who had only arrived in England a year before. It is a gritty play, set in a rundown boxing venue, delineating the lives of five protagonists, all boxers of varying abilities and stages of life and luck. It had a good cast, excellent direction and production and was a very interesting play. It was made into a film which perhaps was less successful as a production than the stage play, with Jack Warner and Robert Beatty.

The cast of both stage and screen productions included George Rose, who became a great friend of mine. He was not unknown for his entertainment of young men backstage. As far as I knew no untoward behaviour went on, he just seemed to like having them around. However, I was duly asked by Hugh Goldie, the Company Manager, if George was indeed entertaining men in his dressing room and, if so, to inform him of this. But when it came to it, I just couldn't bring myself to squeal on a fellow actor who, as far as I could tell, was doing nothing wrong.

George was an excellent actor who spent several seasons playing character parts at Stratford-upon-Avon. Eventually he was murdered in the Dominican Republic by the family of his adopted son. I was devastated when I heard. So very sad and unnecessary.

On to the Town Theatre in High Wycombe. We did two plays, both of which I remember enjoying: *Sweet Madness* and *While the Sun Shines*. For me two things are notable at High Wycombe; one was spotting someone I knew sitting at the end of the second row of the stalls. At the end he applauded loudly and shouted "Oh, well done, old boy, well done." The cast all looked at each other. Who was this chap? Well, he was my grandfather, Arthur Watson who, I don't think, had been inside a theatre for years. The second thing I remember Wycombe for was that there was no prompt after the first night. I was very taken aback by this – they were abandoning us I felt - and asked what if I dried and the answer was that if you remembered all the words for the first night then why would you forget them? Fair enough. In fact I never forgot my lines, ever. Nor did I find it hard to learn them. I have always wondered if the advice from a well-versed and elderly actor, to sleep with the script under the pillow so that the words filtered in your brain through the feathers, didn't have a grain of truth. It isn't only actors who do this, students do it before exams. It sounds like hokum, like a sort of witchcraft – but the psychological fact of placing something under your pillow, especially something that you have been going to bed reading and learning, may have the effect of imprinting what you have read on your brain. Who knows? I did it anyway. And I had no problem with learning my lines. Draw your own conclusions.

So the reps came and went, a whirl of similarities, punctured by occasional real highlights. It might sound like a terrible life but no - it really was not. It was entirely what I wanted to do. I loved the mechanics of the theatre as well as the being on stage. I loved the way it slotted together, the parts that each person played, their being the small cog in the whole. I loved the way everyone pulled together, how we filled the gaps if there was a problem, how – on the whole – we were always there for each other. And all the time meeting new people. But, for my part, never forgetting Pam. We met as often as we could and carried on our romance at a distance with I think a faithfulness that would possibly be derided or at least not understood today. It was a time of tremendous freedom – for me at any rate.

There were two more theatres, Her Majesty's at Brighton for *Top Secret* followed by Leatherhead, though goodness knows what for, and then on to my first television job, *Quatermass*. TV, so it was said, was the up and coming medium, full of bright young things. Who knew what, if any, future it would have? I wasn't at all sure about it but then it had not come my way before. We didn't even own a set – very few people did.

But *Quatermass*, created by Nigel Kneale, who was married to Judith Kerr, author of the Mog series of children's books, was broadcast just at the time when many households had bought a goggle box in order to watch the coronation of Queen Elizabeth. The BBC had hit the zeitgeist in a major way and by golly was it fun! Our director, probably the BBC's top director at the time, Rudolph Cartier, was German and had absolutely no sense of humour which resulted in our corpsing at the slightest thing. It was glorious to be in at the beginning with something so new and revolutionary.

I played a character called Peter Marsh in two episodes. Who was Peter Marsh? What did he do? I'm not sure I know any more. The cast was populated by marvellous people like Isobel Dean, Reginald Tate and Duncan Lamont. All performances were live on a Saturday evening after a full week's rehearsals. A couple of episodes overran – a natural course of events in live shows. I believe that one BBC region cut off the last episode before it finished, something utterly unthinkable today.

I remember a scene in Quatermass when Reginald Tate was about to fly in a rocket to Australia from the grass by Marble Arch and dear Isobel Dean, playing Quatermass' wife, had to say: "Oh, good luck, darling…..and don't forget to bring something home." There must have been about eight of us – all very tired at the end of a long day. We just couldn't help but laugh at Isobel's great line. Rudolph was furious. "Vot is funny? Zhere is nozhing to laugh at…….."

The Quatermass Experiment, 1953. From l. Reginald Tate as Prof. Quatermass, Duncan Lamont as Victor Caroon (under helmet), Isobel Dean as Judith Caroon, me as Peter Marsh and Thorpe Devereaux as Blaker.

And on to Liverpool and the cold copulation……………!

5
Stage Life

Leatherhead and Canterbury 1953

The old Leatherhead theatre (now the Thorndike Theatre) was well run by Hazel Vincent Wallace who also occasionally appeared in supporting parts. We played fortnightly rep, a week in Leatherhead and a week in Canterbury, two companies alternating which, if you come to think of it, is a very good way to run a couple of theatres. The audiences get a fresh play weekly and we, as actors, had the chance to play ourselves in over two weeks and yet not get stale. While in Leatherhead I was able to live with my mother in Cale Street, Chelsea, which afforded us an opportunity to get to know each other rather better. By this time our relationship was more that of sister and brother than mother and son.

With Lupino Lane in *20-1*

When I spent my week in Canterbury I stayed with a most interesting Baroness, who was one of the Cathedral guides, in Cathedral Close. One of my colleagues was that marvellous old character actor, Lupino Lane – best known as Bill Snibson in both the play and the film of *Me and My Gal*, which in turn is famous for *The Lambeth Walk* song and dance.

The Playhouse Liverpool

Although my goal was the West End, I was happy to have one more season of repertory. This time, though, it was three-weekly rep. Liverpool and the surrounding area is large enough to sustain a play for three weeks and, as I said before, it gives us a chance to "bed" in a production. I walked past Liverpool cathedral every day on my way to the Playhouse. This is a marvellous gothic revival building, based on George Gilbert Scott's design and is the third tallest church commissioned, that gothic architecture was the most conducive to prayer and reflection. It certainly does impose on its surroundings and demonstrates the intrinsic might of the church although built several centuries after the height of the Church's overweening and almighty power. But that "power", if not of the Church exactly, but of the power of place, was a culture to which the Victorians still subscribed. Did I find it heart lifting? Yes, indeed, it was heart lifting, for a Church of England Protestant like me. If I thought I was going to be early for rehearsals at the Playhouse, I would pop in and say a prayer or two. The building was certainly impressive. It is, after all, the longest cathedral in the world and overall, the fifth largest.

The Liverpool Playhouse was run by a splendid lady called Maud Carpenter. She did all our contracts and ran all the business side of the theatre: ushers, box office, programmes, bar *et cetera*. But it wasn't long before I discovered that she knew nothing at all about the artistic side of the theatre or even how the business end of a stage is run. I happened to be on the stage after a performance when Maud came through the pass door (the door between the auditorium and the stage) just in time to hear Jonathan Goodman, the stage director, say "All right boys - you can strike now". Maud was horrified. She said "What's the matter, Mr Goodman, aren't I paying 'em enough?"

She held a party in her house once a year in the summer for all the actors and stage management. We would be offered soft drinks, sherry or beer. After a while she came into the sitting room where we were all assembled, clapped her hands and say, "Come along now, that's enough drinking in here. We're all going out into the garden now to enjoy the cold copulation." !

Maud only went on holiday during the summer break either to Bangor in North Wales or to Scarborough in Yorkshire. In fact, except for the Theatrical Managers Association meetings in London, she never went south of the Trent River. One day, though, one of her colleagues in the TMA called her and said "Maud, five of us are going to Venice for a fortnight this summer. Why don't you come with us?" Initially, Maud would have none of it. Go abroad? Oh no. "Venice? No, Jean. Thank you for inviting me, but as you know, I don't do abroad." She did, however, relent under further pressing and, amazingly, enjoyed herself. One of her usherettes heard about the holiday: "I hear you went to Venice, Miss Carpenter. Did you enjoy yourself?" "I did, Jessie. On the first day we had coffee in St Mark's Square and fed the pigeons and went round a church. On the second day we visited the English pub. But the highlight of the holiday was when all six of us went round the Grand Canal in a Lagonda!"

During this time Pam and I barely saw each other. She was working, I was working, and neither had enough money to travel to meet except on rare occasions. We did write lots of letters. It was a pattern we had got used to. But I did buy an engagement ring locally and gave it to her on one of the rare occasions we could get together in London.

On Saturday 25 June 1955 I passed my driving test down near Liverpool Docks. I played the matinee and the evening performances at The Playhouse. On the Sunday I caught a train to London. On the Monday I went to Moss Bros to hire a tail coat and the rest of the outfit for my wedding on Tuesday 28 June 1955 to Pam Marmont. It took place at Chelsea Old Church, that lovely old

building, well known to me since childhood, so it was really the proper and fitting place to be married to my darling Pam. The photograph shows, left to right, Jeremy Fisher, my mother who, I think, had just become newly single from Carlos-Clarke, looking still absolutely stunning, me (looking somewhat debonair even if I do say so and *happy*), Pam looking marvellous as ever, her mother and her father, Dorothy and Percy Marmont, and my new sister-in-law, Patricia, known as Pish, who was then an actress but who later became a very successful theatrical agent, looking elegant on the end. Jeremy Fisher was my best man. I chose him, rather than any of my theatrical friends, because he had been a pal since Eton and he was someone with whom I knew I would always be friends. Dorothy and Percy held a little party as wedding reception after the ceremony in the drawing room on the first floor of their house at 20 Carlyle Square. And we set up our first home as a married couple in the semi-basement there.

When the time was right, some years later, in 1972, Pam and I decided to move to the country. For me, I wanted to go back to Sussex and it was there that we looked. My in-laws owned the leasehold of the house in Carlyle

Square but it was approaching its end of life. They could have stayed until the lease fizzled out and then what would they do? Where would they go? Denville Hall, the actor's retirement home, would have been the only answer because they could never have afforded to renew the lease. There were still a few years to go however and Pish, ever practical, suggested that they sell the remainder, which, because it was in the heart of Chelsea, would be worth quite a lot, even a very short lease. This they did, to a doctor: it had four years to run but it was exactly what he was looking for.

Dorothy and Percy Marmont, with Pam and I at Underwood House

Selling the end of the lease meant that we could pool resources and raise our budget for buying in the country from £10,000 to £14,000. It was an excellent solution all round as Dorothy and Percy could continue to live with us, this time in the countryside. We found Underwood House, on the edge of the village of Etchingham, two miles from the Kent border. Underwood House is a handsome house, not a pretty one, but it came with seven bedrooms and a four acre garden. The Marmonts had a complete wing to themselves, sitting room, two bedrooms, bathroom and kitchen, so they remained independent, but close. Dorothy's sister, Auntie Katie, who worked for a dentist in Cavendish Square, came down often for the weekend as did Pish. I never knew Percy's only son, Jack, because he was killed on active service in WWII, serving on the aircraft carrier HMS Glorious, which was sunk in the North Sea early on in the war.

Underwood House was an extraordinary period in our lives. We were able to receive a variety of friends for weekend visits and have lots of lovely parties. As a new, so-called "celebrity" to the area I was often asked to open local fetes. It then occurred to me that we could have a fete in our own garden to raise money for the Actors' Benevolent Fund.

So, instead of having one "name" opening a fete, I invited my actor friends to come and run the stalls themselves. It was a hoot. We had, for example, Penny Keith, Polly Adams and Patricia Hodge doing "guess their combined weight"; local farmers courteously requesting to lift them up! Robin Ellis and Anton Rogers doing "roll-a-penny", Kenneth More and Peter Bull selling second-hand books, and many others such as Andrew Sachs and Harry Andrews signing autographs. Roger Daltrey, who lived nearby, very kindly brought over his beautifully restored carousel. We once had Adam Faith, known to

Underwood House fete: Andrew Sachs, Patricia Hodge and me with Etricham residents

his friends as Terry, drop in for tea in his helicopter which he landed on the lawn! Happy days!

Just on the subject of charities: most professions have a charity that looks after their own. Likewise the theatre. We have several charities who discreetly take care of theatre folk who need a helping hand. I have been on the committee of The Actors' Church Union and the The King George V Fund, as well as being a member of the Actors' Benevolent Fund. I have recently had the honour of being made Life Vice-President of the The King George V Fund. It has been a privilege to work for these sterling organisations. Long may they flourish.

My father-in-law

My father-in-law, Percy Marmont, had had a good career as an actor. After leaving Liverpool Playhouse, where, years later, I did a season, he took the family to Los Angeles to try his luck in Hollywood. He made several films, the most famous of which was *If Winter Comes*. One of his friends and close contemporaries was Clive Brook who was married to the actress Mildred Evelyn and who had two children, Lyndon and Faith. I would say that Clive and Percy's careers were pretty parallel until the point that Percy got homesick and decided to bring the family back to London. He always said that another strong motivation for returning was that he did not want his children to grow up with American accents! This was not something that concerned Clive. His concern was for his career and, by staying, he became a bigger star than Percy. It is a sad reflection, though, isn't it, that neither of these lovely actors is remembered any more, except perhaps by a few film buffs? Once back in England Percy struggled to find work although he did have a success on the London stage playing the Judge in *Witness for the Prosecution*, presented by Peter Saunders, the great impresario.

Pam and I acted together only once, in a play at the St Martins Theatre (a theatre that overall played a large part in my life) called *Small Hotel* directed by Murray MacDonald, starring Gordon Harker (great uncle of Susannah and Caroline Harker, both well-known actresses today) and Marjorie Fielding. Except for at the Webber D, this was the only time we were on stage together in London. Pam, however, had some success in the West End in *After the Ball*, based on a Shaw play, with music by Noël Coward. Noël said to Binkie Beaumont, one of the outstanding theatrical impresarios of our time: "If all else fails, get Pam Marmont". I have to say that it does sound like a compliment, albeit a bit double edged!

Around this time I met a director with whom I developed a very good working relationship. It is a good thing when this happens because it means that you can rely on a security of understanding. It came about like this: somewhere in the suburbs of London I was in a play that was very well directed by Patrick McGoohan, who was as good a director as he was an actor. Patrick had scored a huge success in Ibsen's *Brand* directed by Michael Elliot at the Lyric, Hammersmith; it had been an absolute triumph for him. Years later he was to be offered the part of James Bond but he turned it down and, of course, that plum went to Sean Connery. Patrick went on to make *Danger Man* and then *The Prisoner* for TV and the latter still has a cult following.

Anyway, for some reason, Jack Minster, director, producer and theatrical manager, came to see this play in the suburbs. I had in fact met Jack previously towards the end of my time at Liverpool: he had asked me to come down to London to discuss a play he was planning to direct and produce. We were to meet in the pub behind the Shaftesbury Theatre where *The Reluctant Debutante* by William Douglas-Home had just opened. *Debutante* starred Celia Johnson (*Brief Encounter* fame), Wilfred Hyde-White and Anna Massey. Although I had not then met Jack before I knew his nickname, "Jolly Jack". You might think this was because he was a permanently cheery, bluff, hail fellow well met sort of person. Ah no. Jolly Jack was lugubrious and appeared to be generally and permanently depressed. Rather an Eeyore. Even though I knew his nickname and why

Broad and Walnut Streets
Philadelphia 2, Pa.

CABLE ADDRESS
BELLSTRAT

TELETYPE 215 569-9703
PEnnypacker 5-0700

12th March 1964.

Dear Moray,

When next you write to Pam, would you please give her a message or perhaps send her this letter. She wrote me one of the very nicest fan letters I have ever had about any play of mine. She, perhaps tact-fully on purpose, gave no address. But I do want her to know what deep pleasure her letter gave me, also to thank her for all the perfectly lovely things she said. I am so sorry I didn't see her, and tell her Graham and Coley too would have adored to see her again.

"The Girl" closes on Saturday - oh well, I must just press on with "High Spirits" I suppose! But it's a great disappointment. I hope you are enjoying your tour, and my love to you both.

AIR CONDITIONED GUEST ROOMS, RESTAURANTS AND FUNCTION ROOMS

A letter from Noël Coward to my wife, Pam

he was thus called, I was still taken aback and amused to find that Jack lived up to his reputation. I congratulated him on the wonderful critical acclaim for *Debutante* that I had read on the train coming down from Liverpool. His reply? "Yes, we are all right for the time being while the 'carriage trade' lasts, but after that - who knows?" Ever the optimist. In fact it ran and ran and was tremendously successful.

So, Jack came to see me in this play directed in the suburbs by Patrick and asked if I would like to be in a play called *A River Breeze* by Roland Culver at the Phoenix Theatre. Culver was also to star along with Phyllis Calvert and Naunton Wayne. We opened in the Lyceum Theatre in Edinburgh and while we were there Phyllis (who was not only very beautiful but an excellent actress) took three of us to an amazing stately home called Mellerstain, about a half-hour's drive south of Edinburgh. This is a wonderful house. I might say that this visit instilled in me a great liking for the stately homes of Britain, with their elegance (mostly) and their decoration, their gardens and their history both of place and of family. Mellerstain had a shop, I remember (nowadays a shop is obligatory, indeed, ubiquitous, at a stately home) where they sold Scottish trinkets and berets etc. I bought a length of tartan cloth for Pam. Isn't it funny that the brain remembers strange tiny incidental things such as the buying of a length of tartan cloth? I can just picture it and feel it in my hands but I have no idea what was made from it.

A River Breeze did not do terribly well and Jack tried to get me out of it because he wanted me for his next project but HM Tennant, the producers, were not willing to release me because to do so would rock an already wobbly ship. So, instead, Jack cast Richard Johnson in the part destined for me in this new work, *Plaintiff in a Pretty Hat* by Hugh and Margaret Williams. Richard, though, was already promised, later in the year, to the Shakespeare Memorial Theatre in Stratford-upon-Avon to play Orlando in *As You Like It* opposite Peggy Ashcroft as Rosalind. However Jack assured me that if "Plaintiff" was successful and likely to run then I would step into Richard's part. It opened in the Duchess Theatre, was a success, and transferred to the St Martins where I duly took over from Richard.

Light comedies were still finding good audiences both in London and in the provinces which meant that they were also well attended by the critics. Tennant's reluctance to let me go from *Breeze* meant that Richard gained the critical plaudits. I will admit to being a bit miffed about missing out on the notices but on the other hand there was some balm in taking over a part in which the original actor was not happy and, sorry to say, the other members of the cast were not sad to see him go either. After the run was over I went down to Stratford to see some friends and while there I visited Richard in his dressing room.

Richard : "You had a good run in *Plaintiff?*"

Me: "Yes indeed"

R: "How did you get on with Hugh Williams?"

Me: "Fine. How did you?"

R: "I couldn't bear it. Couldn't wait to get out and come down here! I used to long to go through that door and say, loudly, 'Dad, the house is on fire!' but I knew he would just carry on smoking his cigarette in his Gerald du Maurier way, so laid back, so underplayed. The public loved him, of course."

After the run in London we did a brief tour with *Plaintiff*. I had left Pam in hospital before I headed off to Oxford. She was expecting our first baby any moment and I had to catch the last train. The stage doorman greeted me with: "Well Mr Watson, it seems you have become a Daddy. The hospital called about 20 minutes ago to say that your wife has produced a beautiful baby girl and they also say you have decided to call her Emma." This was 15 July 1957.

The Grass is Greener

Hugh Williams, known to all his friends as Tam, then wrote another drawing room comedy called *The Grass is Greener* which Jolly Jack Minster again produced and directed. Tam played the male lead and Jack also secured the services of Celia Johnson, Joan Greenwood, Edward Underdown (another old Etonian but older than me by twenty years) and myself to play a manservant called Sellars. Celia was at the height of her fame and was particularly well known to the public for her role in *Brief Encounter* in which she starred with Trevor Howard.

I found the character of Sellars quite difficult to grasp. Nothing I did quite seemed to work. The others had found their parts, all playing pretty much to type. Drawing room comedies in those days were generally typecast. I tried Cockney, I tried a lisp, I tried a limp, I tried sibilance. As a last resort, during the final week of rehearsals (I was cutting it a bit fine), I ventured a Uriah Heep-like earnestness. Celia, who was sitting alone in the fourth row of the Fortune Theatre, just watching the (probably excruciating) proceedings, suddenly shouted "Moray – you've found Sellars!" She turned to Jack Minster and said "Let's do all Moray's scenes all through now and not go to lunch." So we did.

My friends used to say things like "how wonderful to be working with Celia Johnson - what is she like?" I could only answer that I admired her tremendously, like everyone else did. But I hardly got to know her at all. She commuted daily from Nettlebed just beyond Henley¬on-Thames only arriving at the St Martins Theatre in time for the half and leaving immediately after the show. I never went to her dressing room, she never came to mine. When she had time in her dressing room she would work on a huge jigsaw puzzle or finish The Times crossword. We did not socialise. We would speak very briefly when the curtain went up and after the final curtain. As in:

Me: "Goodnight Celia, safe journey home."

Celia: "Goodnight Moray, love to Pam and your children."

Me: "And mine to yours....goodnight!"

Of course she was happily married to Peter Fleming, the great travel writer and brother of Ian Fleming of 007 fame.

My one and only experience of 'drying' on stage came during the run of *The Grass is Greener*. Quite why is a mystery. It happens to the best of us on occasion. One of my friends, Helen Lowry, who was not only a director at the Webber D but an excellent stage manager, was SM (stage manager) for a production of Jean Anouilh's *Ring Around the Moon*, starring Paul Scofield and Margaret Rutherford. About a year into the run, Paul had a week or two of drying and having to take a prompt from Helen. He generally managed to get near her and so, between them, the audience were unaware of this problem. In *Grass* we had been on for about nine months, but, during the day, I had gone back to the Webber D to direct a play, the cast of which included Terence Stamp. He told me he was coming to St Martins especially to see me in the play. I was on at the beginning: just me and Tam Williams. It was about three or four minutes into the performance when the whole play became a blur to me and I collapsed.

Verena Kimmins, our stage manager, brought the curtain down. I had not fainted, just momentarily blacked out. I was saying "I must get back on that stage, I must get back out there". And Tam was saying "There's no need, Moray, there's no need. Your understudy can go on for you." But I said I must get back out there because "I feel like a horse that has refused a fence and I must face it again. I must get back on that stage". Tam relented. We agreed where to start. I had the first line. Up went the curtain and I was nearly thrown again, this time because the audience erupted into loud applause at seeing me back! Happy to say I continued without mishap. The audience is generally on your side and even more so when they feel they have taken part in or witnessed something that is not part of the normal performance. It is that wonderful feeling of collaboration and collusion that makes live theatre so very exciting. Do I miss it? Of course I do!

At the end of the London run we toured to Oxford, Manchester, Newcastle, Edinburgh and Aberdeen, where I was greeted by the doorman who told me I was to call my agent as soon as possible. I did. I had been offered my part in the film of *The Grass is Greener* and would I go to London as soon as possible. I played the week in Aberdeen and left my understudy to continue to Glasgow and the rest of the tour while I hightailed it back to London. Stanley Donen was to direct and Cary Grant was to play the Earl, the Hugh Williams role. Deborah Kerr was to play Celia's part, Jean Simmons was to take Joan Greenwood's role and Robert Mitchum had the part played by Edward Underdown. Wow!

I was called to meet them all in a hotel at the top of Bond Street. Then we had to move to another venue to discuss locations, costumes, et cetera. I found myself going down in the lift with Cary Grant. I offered him a lift in my car which was an almost brand new pale blue Mini Minor.

"Oh how kind of you" he said in that interesting, slightly clipped delivery he had. As soon as he had curled himself into the front seat he said: "How wonderful to have so few gadgets. Our cars in America seem to have dozens and I suppose they are not necessary at all".

Stanley Donen was a very agreeable, laid back director. He had been working on a film with Noel Coward who said to him one day: "Stanley, I hear that you are making a film of *The Grass is Greener*. Why don't I play that butler?" Stanley said he had thanked Noël very much and would think about it. When he saw him a day or two later he said: "I'm afraid I must say no to your very kind offer but I fear it would not be a good idea for Noël Coward to be Cary Grant's butler!"

Stanley was stumped for a butler: the only other Englishman he knew was Raymond Massey who was very busy working in California (where he lived) but who was, in any case, about forty years too old for the part. So Stanley got in touch with Dan, Raymond's son, to pick his brains. Dan was, thank Heavens, a good friend of mine and he just said to Stanley: "Why not use Moray who has been giving one of the best supporting performances in that very play in London for the past year or more?"

So there I am, with all these stellar Hollywood actors.... I got to know Cary Grant quite well because I would go to his caravan on the set at S h e p p e r t o n Studios where we would go through our lines together and sometimes I would hear his lines with Deborah.

Me with Robert Mitchum and Cary Grant in *The Grass is Greener*

I asked him on one of my visits how he filled his time between making films. He said: "I go trekking with two or three chums on horses in the Rocky Mountains. No agents, no wives, no telephones! Wonderful!"

I also asked him if he would go on making films into his old age like C Aubrey Smith. "No," he said, "I shall stop making movies when I no longer get the gal". Mind you, in Hollywood, it doesn't really seem to matter how old the man is, he still seems to get the "gal"! He's allowed to get older but she isn't. Funny that.... One time I was in his caravan and the 2nd assistant director rapped on the door. "Just to remind you, Cary, that you are

lunching with the Duchess of Argyll" (who was at the time a famous society beauty). "So I am. Thank you so much". I watched him go round the corner and then heard him say "Hullo, how lovely to meet you. I'm Cary Grant". Well of course he was Cary Grant. Just one of the most famous men in film making, if not the world. But I liked the way he was so good at introducing himself, American-style, and not making assumptions that one would automatically know who he was.

I got to know Deborah slightly as well. A year or two after we had made the film I chanced to see her in the Royal Academy. She was on the other side of one of their huge rooms being shown round with Rex Harrison. Deborah spotted me and instead of indicating, as she might have done, that she was with a small party and contenting herself with just a wave of recognition, she came all the way over to me to say hullo and ask how I was and how was the family and all that. That was so typical of Deborah. She was indeed a lovely person.

On the other hand I hardly got to know Robert Mitchum. He and Cary were the proverbial chalk and cheese. I got the feeling that Bob rolled into bed at about one in the morning after gambling in Mayfair while Cary turned in at around nine-fifteen. Cary always came to the set looking immaculate, not a hair out of place. Bob - on time, yes - but looking frankly under the weather. But he was a true professional: he always got on his marks and knew his lines. But I had little to do with him in the film, apart from the duel with the pistols between him and Cary which I conducted. Cary was a remarkable man. He kind of reinvented his whole persona. He was born in Bristol as Archibald Leach and in the transition between the west of England and Hollywood he came up with that marvellous mid-Atlantic way of speaking. He was unique. I loved him.

Enough adulation of others - back to me!

Compact! TV!

My agent called me to say the BBC were shortly going to produce a new soap opera called *Compact*. It was about a magazine and they would like me to play the Art Editor. I said to my agent that I hoped he had told them I was not interested. Television

Ronnie Allen, Bridgit McConell and me in *Compact*

was considered a bit *infra dig* back in the early sixties if you were a serious and *respectable* actor and it was absolutely not done to be seen in a soap opera. Ha! Ha! My agent said: "Moray. Sit down and listen to me. For the past ten years you have been playing to 500 - perhaps 1000 people a night. If this *Compact* takes off you will be playing to 5 or so MILLION people TWICE a WEEK!" What could I say? Total *volte face*. "When do I start?"

So for about two years I played Richard Lowe, the Art Editor.

Tuesdays was the live broadcast performance and on Wednesday we taped it for transmission on Thursday. Tuesday was pretty frightening until we got used to it. If you dried you could take a prompt from the floor manager who could press a button (thereby interrupting the broadcast) and quickly give you the line, but he rarely had to. But just occasionally it did feel like a seat of the pants/ got away with it this time / phew that was close / keep you on your toes sort of performance. And the show did go out to millions of viewers. My brother Johnnie was an officer with the Household Cavalry at Knightsbridge Barracks while I was in *Compact*. One day he was walking across Sloane Square in civvies when an old man selling flowers spotted him and said: "Look here, Richard, you were not very nice to Clancy last night were you." For a moment Johnnie had no idea what he was talking about. Then he twigged. He was only a year old than me and we looked very similar but I'm not sure whether he thought it was a good thing to be so recognisable.

Mind you - if you appear in quite a lot of TV you get spotted in the street, in shops and on buses. Yours is a very familiar face to millions of people. They can't always place you. I was walking down Regent Street one day when I saw a man coming directly towards me. He started straight away: "I know your face so well," he said, "I can't think of your name... Hang on... Hang on... It's on the tip of my tongue…. Got it! You're Tony Benn!"

And again, not so long ago, I was in a restaurant and an old lady came up to me. She had white hair, was quite attractive and, I would say, about 75 years old. She said, "Excuse me interrupting you but am I right in saying that you are the actor, Moray Watson?"
Me: "You're quite right. I am indeed."
Old lady: "Oh good! I can't wait to get home and tell my mother I've met you in the flesh. She was a great fan of yours in the early 60s."
Of such stuff fame is made....

When I gave my notice in to the BBC, they asked me how I would like to leave *Compact*.

Above:
with Elspet Gray in *Catweazle*
Dr Who, 1982
The Avengers

Right:
Upstairs, Downstairs, 1972
The Saint, 1964

As James Lees-Milne.   Various stages, various plays.

1959 - A Whitehall farce with: top - Ann Firbank, Dora Bryan, Elspet Gray,
bottom - Brian Rix, myself, Naunton Wayne.

Top: Leonard Fenton, Linda Cooney, Ray Cooney, Emma Vansittart and myself; sitting: Patricia Marmont, Brian Rix.

Bottom: Me, my brothers Michael and Johnnie Watson.

Being presented to Diana, Princess of Wales.

My one man show – *Looking Back and Dropping Names*, with Dancer.

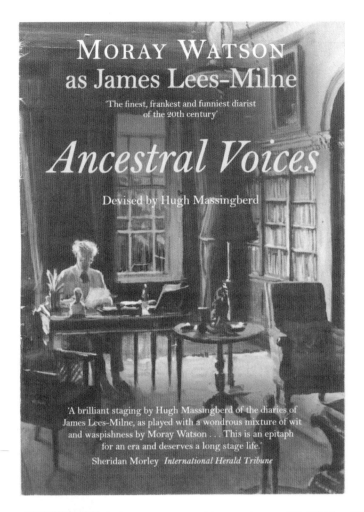

As James Lees-Milne.

A caricature by Al Hirshfeld which was presented to Moray in October 1980. The letter reads:

My Dear Moray,

A small souvenir by way of a thankyou for everything you have done to help make "Nobody's Perfect" be such a success.

It has been a continual joy having you with us & Henry has been a sheer delight.

With love and thanks,
Humphrey [Barclay]

With Prince Philip at the Garrick Club.

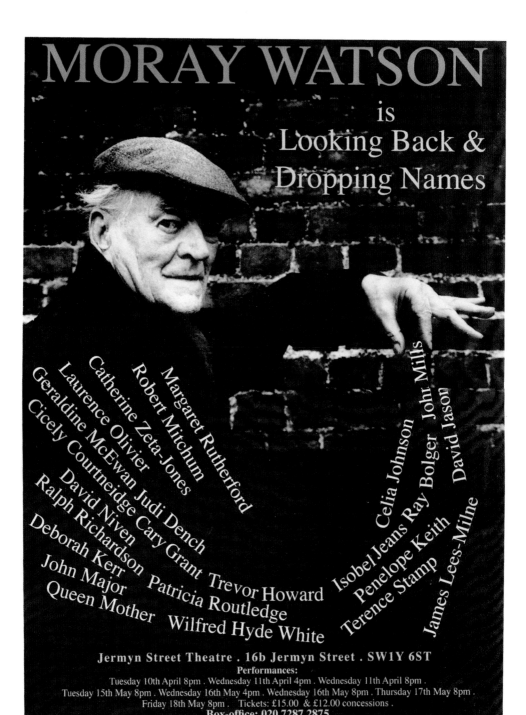

MORAY WATSON

is
Looking Back &
Dropping Names

Margaret Rutherford
Robert Mitchum
Catherine Zeta-Jones
Laurence Olivier
Geraldine McEwan Judi Dench
Cicely Courtneidge Cary Grant
David Niven
Ralph Richardson
Deborah Kerr Patricia Routledge
John Major Trevor Howard
Queen Mother Wilfred Hyde White

Celia Johnson John Mills
Isobel Jeans Ray Bolger David Jason
Penelope Keith
Terence Stamp
James Lees-Milne

Jermyn Street Theatre . 16b Jermyn Street . SW1Y 6ST
Performances:
Tuesday 10th April 8pm . Wednesday 11th April 4pm . Wednesday 11th April 8pm .
Tuesday 15th May 8pm . Wednesday 16th May 4pm . Wednesday 16th May 8pm . Thursday 17th May 8pm .
Friday 18th May 8pm . Tickets: £15.00 & £12.00 concessions .
Box-office: 020 7287 2875

A gift to me from Margaret Rutherford during our run together in *The Rivals*.

Simon Williams, Stephanie Beacham, myself and Amy Williams on tour in *Nobody's Perfect*.

Left:
Me with Rupert
Vansittart, Eden
Vansittart and
the dachshunds.

Below:
with Emma
Vansittart.

With Christopher Timothy in *You Say Tomatoes.*

A publicity photograph.

With Roy Marsden and Michael Elphick in *Pygmalion.*

With Susan Hampshire in *Married Love.*

With Sian Phillips in *Love Affair*.

Beeb: "Shall we kill you off or would you like to work for another company?"
Me: "Why don't I go and lecture in the United States?"
Beeb: "OK. Done. But we may take up an option for you to return to the series at the end."

By chance I did go to America for my next job, not lecturing, but in a Peter Schaeffer play called *The Public Eye* with Geraldine McEwen and Barry Foster. We toured briefly and then opened in New York at the Morosco Theatre. Oddly, there were more English actors in New York that season than ever before. We were all assembled in Times Square for a photograph which appeared in the Sunday Times.

It was November 1963 and I was writing a letter to Pam and partly listening to my little transistor radio. I thought they were announcing a thriller to be heard that evening when I realised they were talking about an event which was actually happening there and then. In Dallas. The assassination of President Kennedy. I called Geraldine:
"Darling, I think President Kennedy has been assassinated"
G: "No darling, I don't think that's very likely"
Me: "Listen to your radio and if I'm right call Roger Stevens and find out if we are playing tonight."

Indeed the theatres and cinemas were closed. But rather than just mope in our apartments we decided to go down to 42nd Street. It was very bleak. Just street lighting. The only theatre that was lit was the one where Charles Boyer was playing in Rattigan's *Man and Boy*. There was a huge photograph of Boyer's head outside the theatre with the lights going on/off/on/off. It was like someone in hysterical laughter at a funeral. Eventually they located an engineer and had them turned off. I watched the funeral with Peter Bull - a good friend of ours from London. He was appearing on Broadway with Albert Finney in John Osborne's *Luther*. Peter was a lovely man. No beauty but with the best of hearts. He used to own a shop, in the 1970s, just off the top of Kensington Church Street, called Zodiac where he sold all things astrological. I think he was extremely interested in matters esoteric – although to look at him you would think it would be down to earth country matters that would take his fancy. He would have been a shoo-in for the part of John Bull, the Georgian "universal" man.

We ran with *The Public Eye* for about five months and then toured briefly to Los Angeles, San Francisco and Denver, Colorado where we played in the American Air Force equivalent of West Point. After the tour I stayed on in New York for a week to thank the friends whose hospitality I had enjoyed. I also saw *Hello Dolly, Funny Girl* and *Dylan. Hello Dolly* starred the magnificent and inimitable Carol Channing who, the night I was there, delivered most of her songs and dialogue to John Gielgud who was sitting in the front row of the stalls.

I saw *Funny Girl* with a theatrical agent that I had got to know. There was some sort of commotion going on while we waited for the curtain to go up. I glanced around to look up at the Dress Circle. There were two or three girls pointing down, straight at me. How wonderful! But looking around I suddenly spotted, two rows immediately in front of me, the slight figure of Ol' Blue Eyes himself, Frank Sinatra. He was with two other fellows. They left in the interval. I assumed they had gone to get a drink in the bar. But no. They had gone. I would have loved to have just said hallo to him. I read in the newspaper the following morning that he had gone back stage to congratulate Barbra Streisand and then had to catch a plane back to Las Vegas where he was performing. *Dylan* was a vehicle for Alec Guinness - a biographical play based on the famous Welsh poet, Dylan Thomas. Actually it was rather disappointing, particularly after the other two. Whether that was Guinness or the play I am not quite sure.

I returned to the UK by boat to Southampton where I was met by Pam, Emma and Robin. After our hugs and kisses Pam told me I had to ring my agent, Larry Dalzell. It seems the BBC had taken me up on my agreement to return to *Compact* for the final six episodes. Fun though that was I was nevertheless anxious to get back to the theatre.

So I was pleased when Larry called to say that I had been offered a good part in George Bernard Shaw's *The Doctor's Dilemma*. There was to be a short tour and then into the Haymarket. Just before it started I ran into Richard Briers in Lower Regent Street. "Hello Moray," he said, "what are you up to?"

Dickie was a good old friend with whom I had toured not so long before in an Aldwych farce. We had been going well but the show folded in Manchester because the leading lady was pregnant and had to return to London. It was *Rookery Nook*, a Ben Travers farce and involved a lot of running about and going up and down stairs. The actress in question had felt ill and gone to see the doctor. He told her that under no circumstances was she to do all the physicality involved in this play and that she should cease forthwith. She came to me in my dressing room and told me. I asked why she had decided to tell *me*. She said: "I didn't think you'd be as angry as Dickie". She was right there. I *was* furious because she must have known when she accepted the part and I found that unforgiveable and unfair on the rest of us, but Dickie blew an absolute gasket. The whole episode was such a pity because the play had been very well received and we had good hopes for a run in the West End.

Me: "Tennants have asked me to be in a revival of *The Doctor's Dilemma*"
Dickie (horrified): "NOT WITH WILFRED HYDE-WHITE?"
Me: "Yes indeed, Dickie, with Wilfred Hyde-White"
Dickie: "He's a monster. He'll destroy you. Especially you. He can't bear other actors getting laughs while he's on stage. Is it too late to back out of it?"
Me: "Yes it is. It's a good part, he's the only surgeon and I'm looking forward to it"

Dickie went away shaking his head. In his view I was heading for the lion's den and obviously going to be eaten alive. In fact Wilfred and I became quite good friends. I often visited him in his dressing room. One night he welcomed me with: "Oh come in Moray. I must tell you that Jack Warner called my agent offering me the part of Colonel Pickering in *My Fair Lady* with Rex Harrison playing Professor Higgins and Audrey Hepburn as Eliza Doolittle. I told my agent: yes I'd love to pay Pickering. Just got to find out if Tennants will release me."
The following evening I visited Wilfred. "Any luck with Tennants releasing you?"
Wilfred: "No. Disaster. I told my agent to get back on to Tennants to find out on what terms they would consider it."

Next night. Wilfred: "Tennants had a meeting with all their directors and they decided they would release me but it would cost me £10,000. So I decided to call Jack Warner myself." I gather the call went something like this: "Jack, it's Wilfred Hyde-White. I understand you would like me to play Colonel Pickering in the film you are making of *My Fair Lady*? Well, as you know I am playing the lead in a revival of Shaw's *The Doctor's Dilemma* in London. Yes. Well the management have had a meeting of all their directors and they have agreed to release me but it will cost me £10,000... (Pause...)... Jack. Are you still there?"
"Yes Wilfred, I'm still here. I'm thinking about it. ...... OK Wilfred, I'll split it with you." And that is what they did! One evening before he left I asked him if he had ever been to a drama academy. Wilfred: "Yes Moray. I did go to a drama academy. I learnt two things: one that I couldn't act and two - that it didn't matter!"

I was playing in *Ancestral Voices*, (about which more later) a splendid one part play written by Hugh Massingberd and based on the diaries of James

Lees Milne. We performed around the stately homes of England and in small theatres all over the British Isles. John Major and his lovely wife Norma came to see it at the Jermyn Street Theatre which is in a small basement at the Piccadilly end of Jermyn Street. It was very well run by a lady called Penny Horner. If you were seeing a play there and knew one of the actors you had to wait on the stage for them to come up from their rooms, which were even further underground. The Majors had asked to see me and were given special permission to come downstairs to do so. I had no idea they were there. I offered them both a drink. Sir John accepted, Norma refused – which was just as well as I only had a mug. They said they had enjoyed *Ancestral Voices* and added that by the way they had been watching me all afternoon. I said that I had no idea I was on TV that afternoon.

JM: "You have been in our house. We've got the whole boxed set of *The Pallisers*." He then asked me when I had been at my happiest and at my most fulfilled during my career.

Me: "I think my two plays at the Haymarket with Sir Ralph Richardson. Shaw's *You Never Can Tell* and Sheridan's *The Rivals*.

JM: "Not *The Pallisers*?" He asked the question quite plaintively. My answer must have disappointed him a bit.

Agents

I started off being represented by Jimmy Fraser. Then on to Larry Dalzell, for fifteen years, who became a good friend. I was also with Ken McReddie, Michael Whitehall and Leslie Duff. Michael has an extraordinary wit. Sharp and quick. He entertained us over many weekends in Sussex, as he now does for millions on prime time TV with his son, Jack.

6
People

I am a gregarious person by nature. Always have been. I am disposed to like people on the whole and do – unless they happen to offend my sense of what is right and wrong – and I don't mean that in a sinful way so much as behaving correctly towards another person. Not taking advantage for instance. I like the morality of correct behaviour. Mind you I am of the old-fashioned school that would never let anyone know I didn't like them. Being gregarious suits an actor and there are many, perhaps the majority, in our profession who are outgoing. We make friends quite easily, some temporary, some lasting, some sporadic, some ongoing (by which I mean we stay in pretty much constant touch). It is in the nature of the profession that it both attracts those who are outgoing and that its ambient nature encourages the participants to be friendly.

So many, many people cross one's path. Each job is likely to bring new faces into your life and for a short period you can become close friends. The intimacy of what we do almost insists on it. It may sound as if I am belying what I have already said about my early years in rep, when I didn't mix so much with the leading lights of the Company and certainly had no idea what was going on in their lives, but I was the new boy and there was then a hierarchy, however small. I think it was only after I finished at Whitley Bay with the Alexander Field Company that I felt that the footing was equal. But all this is a general rule. As you rise, as your star rises, you do find that you begin to work again and again with the same people. A director will have his favourite actors (and designers) and will use them as first choice, always. It is a matter of human nature that we like to make our lives easy and the kind of rapport that is built up over time is important because without realising it you have a shorthand to understanding each other. It doesn't make the play a hit but it might get you closer to the possibility. And as I got older I appreciated being the first port of call.

You knew who you would be working with and so some anxiety is taken away from the process. You knew you would not be having to "try" – and this made things so much easier. When we were first married, living in Carlyle Square, one of our friends was that fine, if a little overweight, actor, Peter Bull who lived round the corner from us at 149 Kings Road. I ran into him when he had just finished making a film and asked him if he had made any new friends. "Oh I forgot to tell you, Moray- " (and I wish I could do his voice in print) "I have made up my mind not to make any new friends. I already have ample and I already spread them too thinly". I often think of Bully now and I do understand what he meant. I think I have ample friends and, yes, "I spread them too thinly". But back then I was still very happy to make a new acquaintance which might turn into friend. It is less easy now - my deafness is an added burden making social interaction less easy, but I am not alone in that. But that is a small digression – I wish to talk about some of the people who have come into my life and stayed, and about one or two who have passed through but who made a lasting impression for whatever reason.

Sir Laurence Olivier

Sir Laurence was living in Brighton and came to see both our plays. For *You Never Can Tell* I was sharing a dressing room with a fine old character actor called Cyril Luckham. There was a tap on the door. It was the great man himself.

"Oh you two darlings!" (This in his Entertainer voice.) "What beautiful performances! Beautiful, beautiful. Thank you so much!" He sort of backed out of our room. He was doing his Archie Rice, his 'humble' acting - straight out of Osborne's *The Entertainer*. It was a part that he had made his own – much to the surprise, I think, of quite a few critics of the time who thought that he was lowering himself by stepping outside the classic theatrical repertoire. But after *The Rivals* his appearance in our dressing rooms took on an entirely different tone.

With Daniel Massey in *The Rivals*

I was in Dan Massey's room giving my impersonation of Larry as Archie Rice in my room the previous year (Oh you two darlings and all that) when Sir Laurence suddenly appears, sweeps past me and proceeds to give Dan a lecture on deportment; how an officer should carry himself. Dan was playing Captain Absolute, son of Sir Anthony Absolute which was Sir Ralph's part. I slipped into my room next to Dan's. In comes Larry and without preamble he begins to tell me what's wrong with my performance. He goes on and on and eventually accuses me of "flirting with the audience". He didn't stay long enough for me to explain what I was trying to achieve or why.

I went off to supper in the Lanes with Dan and Angela Thorne, who was paying Julia opposite my Faulkland and Keith Baxter who was Bob Acres. I was feeling pretty depressed and low after that visit; we were due to open at the Haymarket the following Tuesday. Dan was walking with Angela ahead of me along the Promenade. It must have been about 11.30 and he had had quite a bit to drink. I suddenly heard him shouting "Flirting with the audience? Talk about the pot calling the kettle black!" I was cheered up no end.... Mind you, I'm not sure it isn't part of our job to flirt with the audience.

Ralph Richardson

Through *You Never Can Tell* and *The Rivals* I got to know Ralph Richardson quite well. In *You Never Can Tell* I visited his dressing room after my first entrance and before his. He would tell me who he had seen or lunched with at the Athenaeum Club and sometimes tell me about his early days. One evening he told me that, when he was living

With Sir Ralph Richardson in *You Never Can Tell*

in Brighton aged 17, he went for an audition for the St Nicholas Players, who used a disused factory behind Brighton Station. It was with a Mr Grocot, who was in charge of the Players. Young Ralph felt the interview had not gone too well so he said "Don't be too hasty Mr Grocot. I am a man of means. I will pay you 10 shillings a week for 10 weeks and, if <u>you</u> like me, you can pay <u>me</u> 10 shillings a week for another 10 weeks." Mr Grocot gave him the job. Apparently Ralph's grandmother had left him £100 in her will!

One evening I asked Sir Ralph if he and Sir Laurence Olivier went to see each other's plays. RR: "Oh yes, we generally do, if we are able to." Me: "Did you catch Larry's *Othello*?" RR: "Yes I did see that." Me: "Did you enjoy it?" RR: "Well I rather enjoyed his first entrance. He came on up left smelling a small rose on a long stem. I rather liked that. But after that – I didn't like it too well."

Margaret Rutherford

I was thrilled when I heard that the great Margaret Rutherford was to be playing Mrs Malaprop in *The Rivals*. And as Faulkland (my role) does not have any scenes with Mrs M in the play, I used to go and see her too in her dressing room from time to time. I do remember that at one performance, I arrived downstairs to go on just as Margaret came off the stage, crying.
Me: "Margaret, what's the matter? Why are you crying?"
Margaret: "Ralphie's angry with me."
Me: "Surely not, Margaret."
Margaret: "He is – he's banging his stick on the floor."
Me: "If you forget your lines, Margaret, he'll bang his stick on the floor to help him concentrate on his next lines."
Margaret: "Oh thank you Moray, do you really think so? You are such a comfort to me."

As Faulkland in *The Rivals*

The sad truth was that Margaret was too old to play Mrs Malaprop. It's a hard part to learn even when you are 100% on top of the script. But if it caused some difficulty for those playing opposite her, the audiences still loved her. We all did.

After Margaret left The Rivals, Isobel Jeans took over the part of Mrs Malaprop. Where Margaret's costume was huge and billowing in every direction as a natural accommodation of her body shape, Isobel's was the exact opposite. Twice going past her dressing room I heard her saying: "Tighter, Jean, tighter…" referring of course to her corsets.

Dinah Sheridan and the Windsor Theatre Royal

I loved playing the Theatre Royal in Windsor, especially when I was living in Battersea in Overstrand (which we called Overdraft) Mansions. It was such a quick and easy journey for me. For many years the theatre was run by John Counsell who was married to Mary Kerridge, a well-known actress. In February 1970 I was asked to play a leading role in a play called *Miss Adams Will be Waiting* by Arthur Lovegrove, opposite Dinah Sheridan. What

joy! Dinah was at that time living with the actor, Jack Merivale in Notting Hill Gate. She was extremely beautiful, like an English rose, though in fact both her parents were Russian.

I would often give Dinah a lift to and from the theatre and an upshot of these car journeys together, and of the parts we were playing, was that I became known, by Jack in particular, as "the Windsor lover"! Not true but fun! Dinah was close to her two children, Jenny and Jeremy, by her first husband Jimmy Hanley. Jenny followed her mother into showbusiness and Jeremy became a distinguished politician. He and Dinah were both inveterate solvers of The Times crossword. Jeremy would occasionally call his mother from wherever he was, Westminster, Brussels, Rome: "Have you done 9 across?" "Yes," would come the reply. "*And I'm not telling you!*"

She died in the actors' home, Denville Hall and is still much missed.

The Salzburg Marionettes
John Counsell had invited the astonishing Salzburg Marionettes to perform at Windsor. Hermann Aicher, the son of the founder Professor Anton Aicher, was in charge. They were to perform for one week and eight actors were employed to do the English voices. I was one of them. We loved working with these dedicated brilliant puppeteers.

On Tuesday, Thursday and Saturday evening they performed three items: *Bastien & Bastienne, Eine Kleine Nachtmusic*, which was a concert at Schoenbrunn (with an enchanting Mozart as a boy puppet) and finally *The Dying Swan*. The last was a dance study in memory of Anna Pavlova, who was born in St. Petersburgh in 1885 and died in The Hague in 1931. The music was by Saint-Saens, recorded by George Weigel. This was brilliantly performed by the Aicher family – Friedel, Frick, Gretl and Hermann himself.

I stood at the back of the Theatre Royal to see *The Dying Swan*. It had just started when, a few yards from where I was standing, in came Mary Kerridge straight (and slightly late) from London. She was out of breath and wet but gradually calmed down and became utterly involved with the magic of the unseen Aicher family "performing" *The Dying Swan*. I glanced at her at one point and saw tears flowing down her cheeks. It was an unforgettable evening. The mastery of the Aicher family over the strings of their puppets was remarkable. It is so easy to forget that you are watching a dance composed of wood, paint and string – they have a rare ability to bring the inanimate object to life.

Patric Walker

While we were living in Battersea, Pam and I had the occasional lodger. This was how the extraordinary Patric Walker came into our lives. During his time with us, he met and was discovered by Celeste, the celebrated astrologer. She instantly decided that Patric should become her successor and this he did with great style. Many years later he decided to record his weekly predictions and I become the first voice to read his twelve readings each week. It was quite hard work! Patric stayed a good friend until his early death in 1995.

Alfie Boe

By contrast one who came into Pam's and my life for a short period was Alfie Boe. I first met him when he was a young student at The Royal College of Music behind the Royal Albert Hall. A friend of mine, Tim Ackroyd arranged concerts there to raise money for some of the scholarship students. These concerts consisted of about ten RCM students and ten professional actors. The students played musical instruments or sang. The actors recited poems or extracts from books – and also occasionally sang. I was involved with some of these concerts and when I did the second one, Pam was able to come along. After the show she said  how impressed she had been with the young tenor. She asked me if I had got to know him and would I introduce him? So I did. Although he had a scholarship to the RCM he was almost penniless – indeed he had apparently spent some evenings in Hyde Park with nowhere else to go. He was brought up in Fleetwood some ten miles north of Blackpool and knew no-one in the south. We suggested that he could make use of our attic conversion in our house in Barnes. So he moved in. He fell in love with Barnes and at that point he was determined to buy a flat there. Sadly this has not happened yet. He did achieve, however, his ambition to sing at the Royal Opera House, and then some.

Sometime after Pam died, I went to Glyndebourne to see Benjamin Britten's comic opera, *Albert Herring*, with Alfie in the title role – a role for which, I might add, he won the John Christie award. I went round to see him afterwards and told him that I was about to fly half way round the world, visiting friends and especially relations of Pam's in Australia; starting off in Hong Kong, going on to Singapore, New Zealand, then Australia, Hawaii, Los Angeles and finishing up in New York. Alfie told me, with quite some delight, that he was one of the three tenors playing Rodolpho in the Baz Luhrmann production of *La Boheme* in New York - just at the time I was going to be there. He said he would be delighted to have me to stay in the apartment that the management had promised him. When I was in Los Angeles, I telephoned Alfie to make sure the offer of a bed was still firm. "Oh no Moray," he said, "They promised me I was to have a two bedroom apartment but they have given me one with just the one bedroom. And I have my girlfriend staying with me and my brother is flying in from England. Oh – we have got a puppy staying too!" What a pity, I thought to myself, it could have been fun but then I thought, OK, what shall I do now and it occurred to me that the Garrick Club might have a reciprocal arrangement with some similar club in New York. So I rang them and they did – and I stayed (I think) at the Union Club.

Luhrmann's *La Boheme* was a roaring success and Alfie goes on from strength to strength. He is able to cross the line between opera and musical – one of his triumphs being Jean Valjean in *Les Miserables*. I have not seen Alfie in years but I keep an eye on his career from a distance. It is interesting, sometimes, that you cross paths with someone at certain times in their, or your, life and you develop a closeness which after a time does not continue in the physical and manifest sense but does in a wider empathetic way. It is not quite ships that pass in the night in this case, more that Pam and I were a safe harbour for a while, and for that I am happy.

Kenneth More

We worked together a little, Kenny and I, and it was always a pleasure. Who does not remember his Douglas Bader in *Reach for the Sky*? Or his remake of *The 39 Steps* – taking the Robert Donat part? He played the typical British hero with aplomb in films in the 50s and 60s,

With Kenneth More and Patricia Routledge in *On Approval*

bending the stiff upper lipness into characters with whom one empathised. He alternated these dramatic roles with those of a frothier nature, such as the comedies *Doctor in the House* and *The Admirable Crichton*. I think that, in spite of his success, he has always been a bit underrated. He did fall somewhat out of favour when the kitchen sink dramas came on the scene, but scored a notable hit in the BBC's *The Forsyte Saga* as Jolyon Forsyte in the late 60s.   Kenny was asked what play he would like to do to celebrate the Queen's Silver Jubilee in 1977. He suggested Frederick Lonsdale's *On Approval*. ".… and try to get Geraldine McEwen and Moray Watson to join me." *On Approval* is a four-handed comedy about the notion of trying one's potential partner out for marriage. At least two of the characters are rather unsympatico – and I was one of them. Geraldine was not available so they asked Patricia Routledge, who was. We played a couple of weeks in Birmingham then took it to the Vaudeville Theatre in the Strand. *On Approval* is, I feel, one of Lonsdale's best but I don't think Kenny and Miss Routledge hit it off together too well and I did not think she was right for the part. But – notwithstanding that slight hiccup - we had a nice little run.

Kenny's dressing room in the Vaudville Theatre was next door to mine. Quite early on in the run he popped his head round the door and asked: "Why aren't you a member of the Garrick Club, Moray?" "Me: "Nobody has ever asked me, Kenny." "Well I'm asking you. Who else do you know who is a member?" Me: "Nigel Havers." "Right. I'll propose you and Nige can second me. You'll be in within 3 or 4 years." And I was. It may seem like a long wait but it was worth it and it is not nearly as long a wait as that for a membership of Lords cricket ground!

The Garrick Club was founded in 1831 to "tend to the regeneration of the drama" and provided a haven where, as its first patron, the Duke of Sussex, remarked "actors and men of refinement and education might meet on equal terms". I'm afraid I cannot remember if I had aspired to be a member of the Garrick before then, but I have to say I still am and I still visit regularly. It is a club where people really love to be taken and I will admit that it does have possibly the best atmosphere of any of the clubs in London. It certainly has one of the longest lists of previous members who were prominent in the Arts. So thank you, Kenny! Incidentally – last year, at his father's request, I proposed Benedict Cumberbatch for membership of the Garrick – and not surprisingly – he was made a member within the year: though he does seem to find one or two of the rules of membership somewhat old-fashioned… ..tie wearing for instance!

William Douglas-Home
Thinking about the notion that directors tend to work with the same actors, I have been indebted to Jack Minster for many of my roles. One of these was in *The Bad Soldier Smith* by William Douglas-Home at the Westminster Theatre. William Douglas-Home, was a prolific playwright, possibly most famous for *The Reluctant Debutante*, and brother of Sir Alec (Prime Minister in 1963-4). He spent time in prison as a result of a court martial in 1944 for having disobeyed a lawful command given by a superior officer. He refused to participate, in any way, in the intended wholesale bombing and therefore slaughter of civilians in both Le Havre and in Boulogne. The rules of siege in times of war at that time had not been updated since the days of Henry V and Agincourt, strangely enough. Although the German commander of Le Havre requested permission for the French civilians to leave the city, the British command refused. The thinking was that only total surrender of the Germans was acceptable and to that end all inhabitants of a besieged city or town should remain within the walls as starvation and privation of said citizens could only brig about an early surrender. Douglas-Home thought this unacceptable and refused to obey orders.

He wrote two plays about it. The first, *Now Barabbas*, in 1947 was an examination of his time in prison and I saw this as a Webber D student at the Boltons Theatre (now no longer) in Kensington. In 1961 he wrote *The Bad Soldier Smith* as a justification for his actions during the war. Jack Minster produced and directed a production at the Westminster Theatre and asked me to play Smith, the leading role. The Westminster Theatre was a lovely little theatre on Palace Street, about 100 yards from Buckingham Palace. It started life as a chapel in the eighteenth Century and became a cinema and then a theatre in 1931. It was remodelled twice before being completely overhauled and reopened in 2012 as the St James Theatre. It has a marvellously restored interior, all red and gilt.

At one of the first rehearsals William, who seemed happy enough with Jack's direction and my performance, asked me if I had any reservations about the text. Me: "Not really. Except I do seem to win all the arguments." WDH – unhesitatingly: "I did!"

I suppose he was determined to explain his actions all those years ago and it is interesting that public opinion about the bombing of civilians (then regarded as a necessary evil) has changed quite considerably over the intervening years. WDH did try to get his court martial overturned but did not succeed. The reason given was that the order he was given – to act as Liaison Officer during the siege of Le Havre was not an unreasonable order. He was not being ordered to do anything actively detrimental to life and limb. But I don't think he saw it that way at all. As far as he was concerned, the involvement of civilians as either "punishment" (for crimes committed, supposedly, by one of their number) or merely as collateral damage in bombing or siege and starvation conditions was morally reprehensible.

Terence Rattigan

I want to talk about Terence Rattigan because I think he is up there as one of the greatest playwrights of the 20th century. Perhaps the greatest but each of us has different criteria for what would make the greatest. As I have said, it was his play *Flare Path* in 1942 that set me on my career. It wasn't a sudden *coup de foudre*; all the theatre going and film going had me predisposed to enjoy the notion of make-believe but that particular visit to the theatre was an epiphany. From curtain up I was truly riveted. The dialogue. The acting. The scenery (the 'flare path' itself was outside the window on the set so we could see the planes take off and land). I was not certain then that I wanted to be an actor but I was absolutely sure that that this was a world I wanted to be a part of.

Over the years, of course, I have seen and appeared in plays by Noël Coward, Douglas-Home, Emlyn Williams, Alan Ayckbourn and other twentieth century playwrights but Rattigan still stands out as my favourite of those years. And as a member of the audience I am still in favour of a well-made play with a beginning, a middle and an end. The first of his plays I acted in was *French Without Tears*. I was being interviewed in John Counsell's office at Windsor.
Me: "Surely you must have put on *French Without Tears* before?"

JC: "Oh yes! I put it in every year".
I asked him if he always found an audience for it.
JC: "We'll do about 95% capacity. They love it."
They did. And we did! The leading part I took was originally played by Rex Harrison with Kay Hammond opposite.

I have seen Rattigan's *The Winslow Boy* several times since it opened in the West End in 1946. It always grips me. It involves a family whose young school boy son Ronnie is accused of stealing a postal order. He is questioned by a QC at some length and the family think it highly unlikely that the barrister will take the case. But after the interrogation, rather a ruthless interrogation which reduces Ronnie to tears, the end of the act has the QC saying that he will take the case as the boy is obviously innocent. It is a superb piece of writing.

The Browning Version is a one act play which I have heard people in the world of drama describe as "actor-proof"! I can understand why. It is, again, superbly written and the characters so well drawn that it almost <u>cannot</u> go wrong. Each speech the boy has is spot on as are those of the schoolmaster, Crocker-Harris. I played the Crocker-Harris part at a Festival in the US. I thought the evening had gone pretty well but the next day a member of the audience accosted me in the street and said:
"I saw you in *The Browning Version* last night and I don't think you should be allowed to upset an audience as you did. Men and women were in tears around me."
I didn't know what to say and still don't. But I ask you this. What else is a play for – if not to induce a cathartic reaction in the audience, whether it be tears or laughter?

Rattigan was prolific, as was Coward and as Ayckbourn still is. But what is the test as to which of the middle twentieth century playwrights are the most brilliant? Perhaps it is how often their works get revived after their death. As I write this, the answer seems to be very rarely, which is odd considering how little they date. And I cannot finish this little piece without mentioning Alan Bennett, whose talents and abilities I do admire tremendously.

Terence Stamp – my Cockney hero
Although I was appearing in the West End in the 1960s I had two small children that I was privately educating and thought it would be a good idea to try to earn a bit more money. So I offered my services to my old drama school, the Webber-Douglas. I suggested I could be a stand-by if any of the

staff were sick. Added to this was the fact that when I was a student there I remembered especially the West End actors who had directed me. I went to see the Principal, George Rossiter, who had taken over the Webber-D from W Johnstone Douglas and he engaged me!

I had not been there very long – about four months I think – when Rossiter suggested I direct one of the first year graduation productions and would I choose a play. After considerable thought I decided on Rattigan's *While The Sun Shines*: a play I knew well therefore making direction a lot easier for me. Rossiter gave me the list of young students and urged me to cast them against type to give them more scope. Well. I gave Terence Stamp the part of a young aristocrat, The Earl of Harpenden. Stamp at the time was an East End cockney.

At about 6.30 one evening I was leaving the Webber-D after a chat with George R. It was pouring with rain and it was dark. As I went past the Chanticleer Theatre (part of the school) I was startled by this figure whom I could only just recognise as being Terence.
"Could I have a word with you, sir?"
"Yes. Terence, if you're prepared to walk with me to the Gloucester Road Underground. I'm playing tonight at The St. Martin's Theatre."
While we walked he told me that he was leaving the Webber-Douglas at the end of the term (only his second term) and would I please invite Agents and Casting Directors to my production of *While The Sun Shines*. I said: "No, Terence, I'm not permitted to. It's a policy of the Webber-Douglas to cast against type in the first year. In any case, without being rude, I've cast you as a young aristocrat and, Terence, you have not yet lost your Cockney accent. Aren't you doing a Restoration Comedy with Renée de Vaux? You might ask her."
"Mr Watson, I'm not getting on too well with any of the other directors. Although I may be cast against type, I would prefer an agent or casting director to see me in *your* production."
I did not like to ask him why he had decided to leave the Webber-D early.
"Look, Terence, I'll give it some thought but I must catch my train now."

I did give it some thought and decided to ask his fellow students at our next rehearsal. I gathered them together.
"Listen very carefully," I said, "as you may or may not have realised, Terence Stamp has decided to leave the Academy at the end of this term. As I think you are aware the Webber-Douglas has a policy not to invite agents or casting directors to our productions until the third year. However. I will make

an exception with *While The Sun Shines* provided none of you are against the idea. So at the end of today's rehearsal, if any one of you objects to my doing so, would you please come to me and say so. Thank you. That's all."
Not one came up to me! So I invited two agents and two casting directors. I didn't see the play, of course, because I was playing in the West End.
Next morning I waited with dread for the telephone to ring: an angry George Rossiter sacking me. But I had no call and the subject was never mentioned. Terence got an agent (mine!!) and made a start as an actor.

I remember him calling me to ask if I would help him with a small part he was rehearsing for a play at the Vaudeville Theatre in the Strand. So I invited him over to visit me in Overdraft Mansions in Battersea to teach him a Scottish dialect. But I have no idea what the play was and I don't remember seeing it…..!!

Later on, when I was doing *The Bad Soldier Smith* at the Westminster Theatre, Terence came to tell me that he had an interview with Peter Ustinov for a major role in *Billy Budd*, the film that Peter was directing. I wished him luck and told him to come to my dressing room the following night to tell me how he had got on.
"Well – how did it go?"
"I got the part, Moray."
"You're not serious, Terry – what do you mean 'you got the part'?"
"Well I had to have a bit of a fight with Peter and it seemed to go OK."
"But he didn't actually say 'the part's yours'?"
"No, but I am pretty sure he liked me."
Obviously he did! He did indeed get the part. And the rest? Well, you know the rest. But as a little post script to this: I was in a restaurant in Pimlico with Pam when this chap comes up to me and says:
"I gather you are responsible for Terence Stamp. I tried to get him fired but the producers made me keep him." This was the director of *Far From the Madding Crowd*, John Schlesinger, the film that really made Terence's name.

Charlie Chaplin
The only serious boyfriend Pam had before me was John Herbert, the son of the renowned AP Herbert. AP, born 1890, was called to the bar in 1919 but never practised. He was witty and erudite but it was his wit that prevailed. When he was just twenty he started writing for Punch, the satirical magazine (now no longer with us alas), in 1910. He used his satire over several decades to highlight the absurdities of the law. His *Misleading Cases* became a television series starring the incomparable Alastair Sim as the

judge, Mr Justice Swallow, and the remarkable Roy Dotrice as Mr Haddock. Haddock was a pseudonym that AP sometimes adopted in Punch. He was a novelist, poet, playwright and lyricist as well as a satirist. Among many theatrical successes was his collaboration with Nigel Playfair in the revue *Riverside Nights* in 1926, and, in particular, the hugely successful *Bless the Bride* which ran for over two years from 1947. He became MP for Oxford University in 1935 and was very much instrumental in the overhaul of the divorce laws. AP loved the River Thames and lived beside it in Hammersmith.

After Pam and I married, in June 1955, John Herbert invited us both to watch the Oxford and Cambridge Boat Race his garden in Hammersmith. It became an annual event for us. But the first year we attended the party, 1956, was something special. We duly arrived and John started chatting to Pam. AP suggested that I look at the garden and "introduce yourself to everyone". So, clutching a glass of wine, I go outside. I go down some steps and there at the bottom were two fellows: Field Marshall Viscount Montgomery of Alamein and Charlie Chaplin, just a yard from me and deep in conversation. I dared not interrupt them so went on down to the end of the garden. I reminded John of this incident years later and he said "Oh yes – the Montgomery's are relations of ours and I remember Charlie Chaplin being in London that year and Dad inviting him to watch the Boat Race."

The Queen: Buckingham Palace Luncheon

Out of the blue, I received a card inviting me to "A luncheon to be given at Buckingham Palace by the Queen and the Duke of Edinburgh on Thursday 25th of February 1993 at 12.50 for 1pm". It was one of Her Majesty's "*All Walks of Life*" lunches. In case it seemed appropriate, I took along a photograph I have always treasured of King George VI, Queen Elizabeth, Princess Elizabeth and Princess Margaret Rose arriving at Eton College and being greeted by the Provost, Henry Martin and the Headmaster, Mr Claude Elliott. The King was there to perform an ancient ceremony. An hour or so after a service was held in the College Chapel, and in front of all the boys, the King knighted Henry Martin on the steps of the Chapel. A caption in a newspaper the following day announced "Princess Elizabeth wears her first grown-up hat." Naturally that was the most important snippet of news in the whole event……

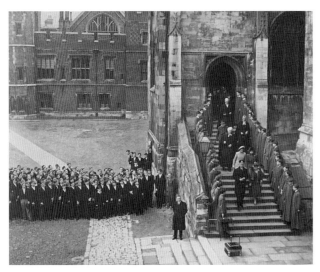
Eton College, 4th March, 1945 Moray is in the front row

We all arrived, punctually as requested, at ten to one. We had barely been there for five minutes when a herd of corgis appeared at speed from round a corner - ahead of Her Majesty and Prince Philip. How many dogs? I lost count after eight. We were not in a straight line, as if for receiving, and so the Royal couple just smiled at us and led the way into the dining room. On my left sat Mr Edward Demery (Clerk of the Royal Cellars) and on my right was Mr Haydon Phillips (Permanent Secretary of the Department of National Heritage). Her Majesty was just beyond Mr Phillips, too far for us to speak. Though she did say half way though the meal, spotting one of her corgis lying asleep on my right foot, "I do hope you don't mind!"

Someone had said to me prior to our visit "I've heard that the food for these occasions is not all that wonderful." But as it happened it was absolutely excellent. At the end of the meal the Queen rose, as we all did, and a lady-in-waiting appeared and said to me, "You haven't spoken to Her Majesty or the Duke, have you?" "No" I answered and the lady-in-waiting said "Do follow her out now".

So I did and proceeded to break two of the fundamental rules of etiquette, certainly of Royal etiquette: first, I spoke to the Queen before she spoke to me and second, I praised the food we had just eaten. Although it is quite *de rigueur* to praise the food of your hosts these days, it wasn't when I was brought up (it was considered such a vulgar thing to do) and it certainly wasn't the proper thing to do at Buckingham Palace either. Nevertheless, I said: "What a wonderful lunch Ma'am."

"Well as a matter of fact, "said the Queen, "We have recently acquired a new chef and everyone, like you, seems to praise his cooking. We had just one reservation about him. He arrived with an Alsatian and my little dogs didn't get on with him so we had to ask him to get rid of the dog. Which he did. The next thing I heard was he then appeared with a Rottweiler!"

At that moment one of the other guests appeared and proceeded to ask the Queen how the repairs were getting on following the awful fire that had damaged so much of Windsor Castle. I have never met the Queen since. I have longed to ask her if she was able to retain that excellent chef. And what happened about the dogs….

Ray Cooney

I have known and loved Ray for over fifty years. He is a brilliant actor, writer, producer and director. We first worked together in farces with Brian Rix in the 1950s. Then Ray cast me in two of his plays, "*Not Now Darling*" and "*Move Over Mrs Markham*", both performing in Johannesburg in the 1970s. He then directed me in his comedy, "Two Into One" with Michael Williams (husband to Judi Dench) at the Shaftesbury Theatre in 1987 and in 1990 he directed me again in William Douglas-Home's *The Chiltern Hundreds* starring Edward Fox. In this production I had the unexpected pleasure of playing opposite Judi Dench's delightful daughter, Finty. Our characters ended up engaged to be married!

Every year Ray and his lovely wife, Linda give an amazing Summer party at their home in Epping Forest. They very generously invite everyone that they have ever worked with including everyone's wife, husband, children, grand-children and dogs! It is always a joyous occasion. A band plays while we queue for delicious puddings alongside the likes of Maureen Lipman and Tom Conti. Ray is always a joy to work with and is and was such a staunch friend to Pam and me.

Penelope Keith

Penny and I first met in the 60s when our mutual friend, Barry Justice, brought her over to our home in Battersea.

She and I were later to appear together in *Miranda* at the Chichester Festival Theatre and also in *Hay Fever* at the Queen's Theatre. Penny has, for many years, been a marvellous president of the Actors' Benevolent Fund.She is the only person who calls me "Mo". I adore her.

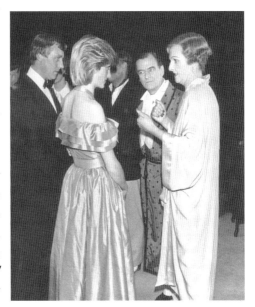

With Penelope Keith in *Hay Fever*, being presented to Princess Diana

Penelope Keith and I in *Miranda*

Judi Dench

Judi and I first met doing a play for ITV television in 1968. A glorious four hander by Fredrick Lonsdale called "*On Approval*" starring Maggie Smith, Robert Stephens, Judi Dench and myself. Maggie and Robert, I think, were engaged at the time which meant that Judi and I were somewhat thrown together. This sealed a lifelong friendship. I remember once, during time off from rehearsals, we were walking near Shaftsbury Avenue together when Judi suddenly said to me "There's a postbox! Can you post this letter for me?". Bemused as to why she didn't just pop it in herself, I obeyed.
Judi: "There now. I've GOT to do it!"
Me:"Do what"?
Judi: "'*Cabaret*" .They want me to play Sally Bowles! It's terrifying, I've never been in a musical before!"'

From r: Finty Williams, John Moffar, Judi Dench, Martin Tickner, Emma Vansittart; Whitehall Hotel, Lincoln, October 1990.

Needless to say she was sensational. This production set her on the path to becoming one of the leading actresses of our day. However Judi now refuses to work with me ever again as our corpsing becomes too outrageous!!!!!

And from the sublime to the homely – my own Summer Garden Parties. For fifteen years I had an annual party in my garden in Barnes. It came about in a slightly unusual way.

My friend, Adam Woodroffe, whose garden in Clapham I had attended to in a small way, had just moved to a ground floor garden flat in Queen's Park with his friend Hamish Clark. A week or so later he invited me over to have a look at it and enjoy some coffee. Adam was busy at his desk when I arrived with one of the latest electrical toys – a computer.

"May I look round the garden?" I asked.

"Yes, of course," he said, "but there's nothing to see. It's all thistles, nettles and weeds. So while he put the kettle on, I decided to wander into the garden anyway. Of course – he was quite right. It was rubbish. Over coffee I said:

"Would you like me to do something about the garden?"

"Well, yes, great, if you can spare the time."

And to cut a longish story short, I set to work. Within days it was looking … … well – at least clear of all the nettles and thistles. I bought some roses and plants and it was really beginning to look like a garden, albeit a very small one. I had spent about £150 on the roses and flowers. Adam said "I'll pay £50, Hamish can pay the same. And I think I will call the landlord." He did – and I heard him saying "Yes, he's a professional gardener!" (Crossing his fingers.) "Thanks very much." There was much laughter as he told me that the landlord would also contribute £50.

We celebrated with a little lunch party. Two girls were running up lunch in the kitchen and four chaps were finishing off in the garden. "We should have this party every year," I said. Adam said that the garden was not really big enough to

host a proper party. "Right," I said, "we'll have it in my garden in Barnes, which, even though it is only a small garden, is twice the size of yours."

So every summer for some fifteen years I had an annual garden party for about twenty-five of us. And a very happy time it was too. I have a collection of framed photographs depicting each and every one of them. Good memories.

JANE DOWNS

JANE DOWNS

JANE DOWNS, who plays Diana Lake in "French Without Tears", has appeared in five West End productions since she won the Gold Medal at the R.A.D.A. and earned a two-year contract with H. M. Tennent. Her first play was the amusing comedy about income tax—"Both Ends Meet"—which ran for nine months at the Apollo Theatre. Then followed "Patience", in which she played Geraldine McEwan's sister, but unfortunately the show never reached London. Her next appearance was in "Lucky Strike", with Ambrosine Phillpotts, and last Christmas she played in the highly successful revival of "Charley's Aunt" at the Globe, with Frankie Howerd in the lead. More recently Jane played Fiona in "Salad Days" while the London company had a two weeks' holiday, and she has only just finished in "A River Breeze" at the Phoenix Theatre.

MORAY WATSON

MORAY WATSON made his first appearance at the Theatre Royal, in the auditorium as a schoolboy in 1944. After that several "special occasions" were celebrated by trips to Windsor and the theatre. He left Eton in 1946 and went into the Army and so to Drama School. He remembers wondering as a schoolboy if he would ever be "up there" entertaining, instead of being entertained, and now happily, 12 years later, "a wildest dream" is coming true, and Moray Watson will be the other side of the footlights—playing the Hon. Alan Howard in "French Without Tears".

The years between have been spent in broadcasting, television, filming, touring and playing in repertory up and down the country. In London he appeared in "Small Hotel" with Gordon Harker, Marjorie Fielding and Pam Marmont (his wife), and he recently played in "A River Breeze" with Jane Downs.

MORAY WATSON

7

As Seen on TV....

I have done a pretty decent amount of television work, which has been fairly constant since the *Quatermass Experiment* in the early 50s. Of course, when I started out in this glorious profession, the apogee was the West End stage and the plaudits gained from good notices. Besides which I just loved the whole process of theatre craft. Also television was regarded, as I have said before, as a medium for those actors who could not "make" it on the stage! It is quite astonishing to think of that now, what with the demise of the repertory company and the rise of TV stardom. I could not have foretold it, although others did. And I am grateful for my agent having pushed me into *Compact* – in this way I did reach millions of viewers, far more, of course, than I ever would in several stage lifetimes.

Being in the TV studio was a different sort of seat-of-the-pants experience; at least it was then, when episodes were transmitted live. And you had less rehearsal time too. If you made a mistake it was not so easy to cover but, as in any live performance, you just had to continue. There was no stopping to re-record and no post-production editing to make the programme fit into the allotted time slot. Indeed, I have talked about *Quatermass* overrunning its time slot and being cut off before the end. *The Quatermass Experiment* was one of the first television series made for mass entertainment. It came out in 1953, the year of Queen Elizabeth's coronation and as I have said, many households had invested in a brand new television. On reflection they probably did not buy the box outright but rented it from shops like Rumbelows, now long gone.

The author of *Quatermass*, Nigel Kneale, wanted a name that was memorable and striking. As a Manxman, he was interested in the fact that many of the Manx islanders had surnames beginning with "Qu" so he trawled through the telephone book and found Quatermass. The character he invented could be described as Britain's first hero. It is fun to look back knowing that I was associated with something as pioneering as that.

Then, of course, came *Compact* – about which I have already written. This was also fun to do. It was in direct contrast to the grittiness of *Coronation Street*, being much more "middle-class". Someone described it as being an early "avarice" soap which I find rather funny. But yes, I think it was!

In between *Compact* and *The Pallisers* I was in *Thirty Minute Theatre*, *The Sunday Play*, *Catweazle* and in episodes of *Z Cars*, *Dr Finlay's Casebook*, *The Saint*, *The Avengers*, *Upstairs Downstairs*, *Tales of the Unexpected*, *Doctor Who*, *The Professionals*, *Miss Marple*, and many, many more – all the usual suspects.

The Pallisers

The Pallisers was a large undertaking by the BBC with two series of thirteen episodes and a huge cast of actors. It was produced by Martin Lisemore and directed by Hugh Dowd and Ronald Wilson. Susan Hampshire was already cast as Lady Glencora. Martin, I gathered from Larry, would have been happy with either me or Philip Pearman playing Plantagenet Palliser. He decided to leave it to the director of the first thirteen episodes to make the choice of actor for Planty Pal. Alas for me at the time, Hugh chose Philip Pearman.

Larry Dalzell called me to break the news. Good news and bad news he said. He gave me the bad news first which was that Planty Pal had been snitched by Philip Pearman. The good news was that the producers had offered me the part of Barrington Erle, the leader of the Liberal party, and as such, would appear in half the series. Whereas Planty Pal would not. So in the end, even though the part of Planty Pal had women swooning over him (even recently someone said "Oh Planty Pal, he was gorgeous"!), I had the more exposure as Erle. And Larry and I had both gathered that this production was to be a pretty prestigious series and it would be good to be associated with it. So we accepted the offer.

In the first few episodes a great friend of Pam's and mine, Barry Justice, was playing Burgo Fitzgerald. Burgo was madly in love with Glencora and nearly ran away with her but she was also involved with Planty Pal who persuaded her to leave Burgo altogether. Our friend Barry was great fun and very popular but he was a homosexual, which he hated, and was also upset that he had not already become a star by his late 30s. Peter Bull, who was a mutual friend, telephoned me several times to tell me that Barry had called him more than once saying that he wanted to commit suicide. "I go over to him to calm him down. You're lucky, Moray. You live in the country (we were at that time living in Etchingham in East Sussex) otherwise he'd be calling you."

From top left:

Catweazle

As George Frobisher with Leo McKern
as *Rumpole of the Bailey*

Mr Bennet – *Pride and Prejudice*

The Brigadier in *The Darling Buds of May*

Donald Pickering, Derek Godfrey
and me – *The Pallisers*.

Poor Barry. He did take his life a few weeks later. An estate agent was showing a young couple round his flat off Gloucester Road. By chance my daughter met this poor estate agent a few years later. He was obviously devastated by discovering the body but was moved to note that Barry had amazingly considered whoever would find him by placing a cardboard box over his head to limit the horror. Barry had shot himself in the head. We all were horrified. Such a lovely man, such a good friend and such a terrible waste of life.

I also had the joy of being Mr Bennett in the 1980 BBC production of *Pride and Prejudice*, with Elizabeth Garvie as Lizzie Bennett and David Rintoul as Darcy. And the fun of being Judge Frobisher in the wonderful *Rumpole of the Bailey* with Leo McKern. Oh - and *Minder* and *Yes Minister*!

The Darling Buds of May
I was so pleased to be asked to play the Brigadier in *The Darling Buds of May* for TV in 1991. It was a rollicking dramatization of HE Bates' novel, and its sequels, and was about the lives and loves of a rural farming family, the Larkins. David Jason and Pam Ferris were Ma and Pa Larkin and the as yet unknown Catherine Zeta-Jones was their older daughter.

As befits such a bucolic tale, the series was mostly shot outside, in the village of Pluckley, in East Kent. We were lucky in that the weather throughout was glorious. My house, the Brigadier's house (or the "General" as David would sometimes refer to me), was right in the centre of Pluckley. This village has the reputation of being one of the most haunted villages in England. At Hallowe'en they lay on extra police to cope with all the people who descend on the place with recording machines and home-made ghost catching/sighting traps.

One day I had a scene walking up to "my" front door. My arrival at the front door coincided with the actual owner's arrival home. I asked him if his house was haunted. He replied that "…it had been. I came home one evening and saw my wife at the first floor window. She opened it and shouted down to me 'If you don't get this house exorcised before Christmas, it will be grounds for divorce.' Well, of course I got the vicar in and he went through every room, telling the spirits to go away. And they did."

On another day we were filming a gymkhana and Catherine appeared on horse-back looking absolutely immaculate. Black hat and jacket, white stock and pin. But I was aware, as she trotted into the ring, that she did not look comfortable, staring down in front of her and holding the reins too tightly. And horses can always tell if a rider is inexperienced and nervous. This one certainly did! It started cantering out of the ring and into the countryside. It jumped a small brook in the process throwing Catherine off. She was rescued, a bit grass-stained, and driven to hospital. No great damage, mercifully, except perhaps to pride. The following day I saw her and said: "Catherine, I saw you riding into the ring and I had a feeling you were inexperienced." Catherine: "I'd never ridden before, but I knew a stand-in was going to do the jumps so I hoped for the best. When I auditioned for the part and they asked me if I could ride, because there would be a gymkhana in one of the episodes, I just said 'yes'. Otherwise they might have cast someone else".

We all do that, as actors, fill in forms and questionnaires and say we can do things when we have had no experience of playing squash or parascending or even riding a horse. No lack of talent, ability or expertise in any area is going to prevent an actor going after a part! Mind you I have never been asked to ride a motor-bike or swim under water, which were skills that I had ticked when I joined my first agency.

The timing of the broadcast of *The Darling Buds of May* could not have been better. For some reason it rode the wave and the TV watching audience lapped it up. It broke records. A second series was called for. But this time we did not have Pluckley to ourselves. Our fame was such that a chap on the local radio station suggested that "instead of taking the kids to Margate or Ramsgate, why not take them to the beautiful village of Pluckley and watch the filming of *The Darling Buds of May*. And the local population appeared to do just that. Consequently the filming of the second series took rather longer than intended as herding the general public and exhorting them to be quiet and hold still while shooting is a very time-consuming occupation.

David Jason and I had a scene on the terrace of the village pub overlooking the village square. We went out to play our scene and were confronted by what must have been a hundred families out there, all with buckets and spades and cameras and autograph books. Unlike a theatre audience which understands the need for silence so the actors can play their scenes, this kind of on-looking audience needs to be told to be quiet, please, and not use cameras or make any noises when "Action" is called. But inevitably there is always a baby bawling or some fool who thinks the request does not apply to him so we are brought up short and have to begin again. Popularity is a two-edged sword in this kind of situation. On the one hand you are immensely pleased that what you are doing is appreciated and liked – on the other hand it makes it extremely hard just to get on with the job in hand and acting is a job, like any other. It is just that it appears to be a more glamorous way of life than many people experience. Understandably they want a bit of it, and of you.

Yorkshire Television, YTV, was keen for us to do a third series and discussions were held about it. But the notion was a tricky one, mostly because they had run out of the original HE Bates storylines and it would mean having to bring in a writer to create stories that suited the various characters. In the end they decided not to and I think they were right. We finished on a high note and most of us all found work after Darling Buds quite quickly.

During filming I asked Catherine what she wanted to do next and she said "I want to get back to my singing. I've done a couple of musicals in London in a quite minor capacity but I'd like to do more." In fact, a decade or so later, she went on to play the part of Velma in the film of the musical *Chicago* and won an Oscar as Best Supporting Actress. She also met and married Michael Douglas, son of Kirk "I am Spartacus" Douglas.

Since then I have been in episodes of *Dangerfield, Kavanagh QC, Midsomer Murders* (like everyone else!) and *The Vicar of Dibley*. I was in one episode of the V of D. Larry Dalziel called me to tell me that BBC TV would like me to be in their successful series of the Vicar of Dibley, starring Dawn French. I asked if they were to send me a script.
"Well, no, Moray. There's not much point because you only have one line."
"Larry, I really think you must get back to them and say no."
"That's what I thought you would say but they got back to me and said 'Would you tell Mr Watson that we are offering £1000 for the one day's work?'"
"OK, Larry, book me….!" Well, you would, wouldn't you? It is not always like this, though, believe me.

Films
I have talked about *The Grass is Greener* with Cary Grant and I have only been in a couple of other films. The first was *Operation Crossbow* which starred Sophia Loren (no, alas, I did not meet her…!) and George Peppard. It contained all the other actors you would expect to see in a war film of the time: Trevor Howard, John Mills, Anthony Quayle, Paul Henreid, Pat Wymark, Richard Johnson Maurice Denham, John Fraser: I could list them forever and each one would be a name we all know. Lovely to work in such illustrious company! I do not remember much about it, but one thing sticks in my

mind. I recall this one scene where most of the actors were surrounding a huge map about 6 yards long by 4 wide. We had not gone to our dressing rooms to await the start of the scene because this particular scene did not require any subtle lighting changes. I was at the end of the table when Trevor Howard sidled up to me and whispered: "Have you noticed that nearly all the others are wearing lifts?" Two of them were John Mills and John Fraser; both in need of any means to make them look taller!

Operation Crossbow

What I like about this story, *non-sequiter* as it might seem to be, was that Trevor Howard must have noticed that I was nervous and a remark like that is bound to put another actor at his ease. It also demonstrates, and embodies, the "naughtiness" that actors are prone to.

The second is *The Sea Wolves* which starred Gregory Peck, Trevor Howard, David Niven and Roger Moore. I was on it for two weeks in Delhi and then six weeks in Goa. It was based on a true story and concerned an episode very early on in WW2 when two vast German ships found themselves in the Indian Ocean when war was declared. They decided to make haste to Goa because it was neutral, thinking that they would only be there for a few weeks until the war was over.

However, as the war dragged, they got bored doing nothing, so they started sending signals to their submarines, telling them where our ships were in the Indian Ocean. This, of course, was illegal. So the British powers called London and asked them what could be done about it. Churchill replied, in so many words, "I'm very busy so try and sort it out yourselves." And that is what happened.

They rallied the Calcutta Light Horse who were enjoying themselves boozing and playing Polo. A number of them took the train down to Cochin where they boarded a barge – not unlike a Thames barge – and progressed up the West coast of India to Goa. Their mission was to board and destroy the German ships. Which they did. Everyone was under strict instructions not to breathe a word, not even to their wives, of what was about to happen.

Gregory Peck, the most agreeable man, was in overall charge of the British. David Niven was in charge of us on the barge. In one scene I was standing

Top: *The Sea Wolves*, I'm second from the right in the middle row.
Bottom: On a polo pony, Goa, 1979

next to David – it was quite windy – and I was sick all over him. Actually this was part of the filming. I remember I had to fill my mouth with a mixture of Heinz type food and at the right moment be sick. Most of it, with thanks to the wind, all over David….

 While the actors were in Delhi we were asked to hold up a hand if we could ride. Up went mine and about three others. And then for three days we were taught the art of playing Polo! We were lent (how very kind and trusting of the owners) some experienced Polo ponies who seemed to know exactly where the ball was and how best to get the rider to it. It is an exhilarating canter across the Polo field, wielding a mallet – and when you actually hit the ball, when you capture exactly the right angle and whack the ball out of existence, there is such a great feeling of elation, of man and horse and arm and mallet in superb co-ordination. Incredibly enjoyable – and FUN!

The most boring aspect of filming is the long wait to be called for your scene. Maybe you wait in your dressing room, maybe you wait on a seat on the set – just waiting for your scene to be lit. We were lucky enough to have six bridge players among the cast of The Sea Wolves…. So, whenever possible, four of us would play with two on standby. If one of the players was called away – there would always be someone to fill in and we would issue an instruction such as "We're playing 3 spades, diamonds are trumps. Good luck!"

8

One Man Shows

The Incomparable Max

To a certain extent my career as an actor started off conventionally: ie drama school, lots of rep, plays in London, touring, films, TV. Where it becomes not so conventional is when I started to do one man shows. When I set out as an actor, I never gave a thought to playing to an audience ALONE! In fact I always thought of myself as a *team* player. It was in the early 60s that I thought it might be a good idea to have a one man show up my sleeve to do between plays and TV work. And indeed it is not often that an actor will finish one job on a Saturday night and start the new one on Monday morning. Sometimes the waiting in between is because there is nothing around that he is right for. Sometimes the next job offered wouldn't be satisfying.

There are any number of reasons – including the need for a holiday! He needs the money, of course. I have only ever known one actor who had enough money not to work at all! But I do not like hanging around for the next job to come along so I started to consider planning a one-person performance. I set my mind to it and came up with several ideas. Somerset Maugham was one – there were a couple of others which I remember thinking were rather good, but I can't for the life of me remember what they were now. Was George Bernard-Shaw one of them? I don't remember. I mentioned these ideas to my friend Sheilagh Ward Ling who lived in Hastings. She, albeit politely, told me I would be quite wrong for any of my ideas. And I had wracked my brains till they hurt. So I told her.

I may have been slightly tart for which I am sorry, dear Sheilagh, to come up with some alternatives. She obviously mentioned our conversation to her husband, Peter, because a few days later he woke Sheilagh up in the middle of the night: "Sorry to wake you, but I may have forgotten in the morning. I know who Moray must do a one man show about. Max Beerbohm." Funnily enough we had recently been talking about Max Beerbohm but not in this context. I did wonder aloud whether there would

[98]

be enough material. Sheilagh set to work on it and within days she was saying things like: "It's not a question of there being enough material; it's a question of deciding what to leave out." Sheilagh started on composing the initial script. Between them she and Peter did a splendid job on *The Incomparable Max*. So that's how my first effort began... Max Beerbohm 1872-1956 is a fascinating subject. A theatrical man in all senses of the word: half brother to Sir Herbert Beerbohm Tree, the great actor, artist and impresario. Max took over from George Bernard-Shaw as Drama Critic of the Saturday Review. He was most famous for his caricatures, but he wrote many books and one delightful novel called "*Zuleika Dobson*", based on Oxford undergraduate life.

Herbert was nearly 20 years older than Max and when Max came down from Oxford, Herbert asked him if he would like to accompany him, and be his part-time secretary, on a tour he was planning across the United States. Max, who had no immediate plans, accepted. When they reached Philadelphia, Herbert said to Max that that there was not much more Max could do for him there and why didn't he go on to New York, see a few shows and they would meet in a couple of weeks' time. Max, again, readily accepted. "Oh, by the way, Max, see what you like and think that you will enjoy, but would you see one play for me called *Trilby* which is causing some interest up there and let me know what you think of it?" Max saw *Trilby* and his report back to his brother was unequivocal. The play was absolute nonsense and was bound to be a resounding failure were Herbert to be so ill-advised as to produce it in London. Herbert was well known and feted in New York but in spite of his celebrity status he found himself with nothing to do on his last day in New York and so went to see *Trilby* himself. He bought the play immediately, produced it at the Haymarket – playing Svengali himself – and it became a raging success. Tree used the vast profits from the play to build the magnificent His Majesty's Theatre over the road from the Haymarket. Incidentally – Tree produced the very first production of Bernard Shaw's *Pygmalion*; he played Professor Higgins; Mrs Patrick Cambell (she who praised the comfort of the double bed after the hurly-burly of the chaise-longue) was Eliza Doolittle and Philip Merivale played Colonel Pickering. They opened at His Majesty's on 11th April 1914.

I asked the TV director John Gorrie to help me – in fact to direct me in *The Incomparable Max*. I had decided to learn the whole script before we started. John would come to our house at Etchingham in Sussex and we would rehearse in the long drawing room. He was very helpful but I remember that it was about 12.45 one afternoon when John stopped me and said: "Moray – why do you keep looking out into the garden?" I replied; "I was hoping, John, that someone might come in and join me." John, laughing, said: ""I think we had better join Pam in the kitchen and have some lunch". It was a strange and lonely process at first. I was used to dialogue with someone else for goodness sake – not a long monologue. It took me some time to accustom myself to being happy with my own company on stage – or even before I actually got to the stage – there's a sort of trick, I think, whereby you con yourself first into believing you can hear the other voices and then it becomes second nature to hear the other unheard voices, the

other invisible characters which make up the one man show. No man is an island and all that. The best one man shows deliver an all round performance: by which I mean that as well as the character one is portraying, one should include, within the performance, various elements of other people with whom your character comes into contact.

A kind of alchemy. I launched *The Incomparable Max* on the stage of the theatre in Sussex University and then on and off over the next year I toured round the Home Counties. I played it whenever possible between the jobs that Larry Dalziel fixed for me.

Pam and I had got to know a woman who lived near us called Maureen, Marchioness of Dufferin and Ava who "came out" (as debutantes, not as gay!!) at the same time as the Queen Mother. Every year Maureen would host a dinner party for the QM in her London house, between Sloane Street and Harrods. As well as inviting the aristocracy, she always included one or two actors, singers and dancers. She very kindly invited Pam and me. It was a rather bleak winter night as we arrived, as directed, at 9 pm. A housekeeper let us in, saying "The gentlemen are still in the dining room, but please go upstairs where you will find Lady Dufferin and all the ladies, including Her Majesty." Up we went and sure enough there was Maureen to

ALGERNON SWINBURNE

FRANK HARRIS

MARQUIS OF QUEENSBURY

AUBREY BEARDSLEY

OSCAR WILDE

MORAY WATSON
AS

Sir Max Beerbohm

REMEMBERING FAMILY, FRIENDS AND ACQUAINTANCES

**SIR HERBERT BEERBOHM TREE • AUBREY BEARDSLEY
FRANK HARRIS • HENRY JAMES • RUDYARD KIPLING • DAN LENO
WILLIAM ROTHENSTEIN • BERNARD SHAW
ALGERNON SWINBURNE • OSCAR WILDE**

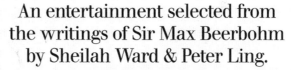

❖ ❖ ❖ ❖ ❖ ❖ ❖ ❖ ❖ ❖ ❖ ❖ ❖ ❖ ❖

An entertainment selected from
the writings of Sir Max Beerbohm
by Sheilah Ward & Peter Ling.

The setting is the terrace of Max's villa in Rapallo near Genoa.

The first half is in the summer of 1930: the second half is an
autumn evening in 1955.

❖ ❖ ❖ ❖ ❖ ❖ ❖ ❖ ❖ ❖ ❖ ❖ ❖ ❖ ❖

HENRY JAMES

BEERBOHM TREE

BERNARD SHAW

RUDYARD KIPLING

MAX BEERBOHM

greet us. Pam immediately fell into conversation with the Duchess of Northumberland, as you do. Maureen said to me "Do you know Reresby Sitwell?" Me: "Yes, I do" "Well," she said, "you are next to speak to Queen Elizabeth. So look out for me, because when she looks as if she had had enough of Reresby, I'll take you over to meet her. By the way, am I right in saying that you were at Eton with Fergus Bowes-Lyon?" Me: "Yes I was." "That's how I will introduce you then." So – over we go. Queen Elizabeth, who must have been about 90 at the time, was lying on a chaise-longue. I sat by her feet. "This is Moray Watson, the actor, who was at Eton with your nephew Fergus." "Oh!" says the Queen, "which of us was lucky enough to see him last?" And we were off. She very kindly asked me what I had been up to and assured me she had seen me many times. We chatted away for about ten or fifteen minutes and she finally asked me what I was going to do next. "Well, ma'am, next week I am going up to the Edinburgh Festival to play my one-person play *The Incomparable Max.*" "How splendid" she says "and do you know where you will be playing it?" "Oh you wouldn't know it ma'am. I'm going to be in the Wax Museum." "Know it?" she said, "I'm IN it!" Followed by much merry laughter…

One little side note regarding my old school chum Fergus: once a month, in one of the grander rooms of Buckingham Palace, the entire Royal family would meet for tea. On this occasion, Fergie, then aged about 7 or 8 was present and seated next to the Queen (later our Queen Mother). After the champagne was poured out Fergie discreetly got out his pen-knife and started stirring his glass. "What are you doing?" whispered the Queen. "I'm getting rid of the bubbles" he replied. "Well, it's alright here but what would you do in polite society?"

After my two weeks in the Wax Museum with Max, Pam and I decided to have a break. We were interested to see the house that Beerbohm retired to, at the early age of 40, in Rapallo in northern Italy. We duly booked into the Hotel Italia and Lido. We met, and subsequently spent some time with, a charming couple, Professor Massimo Bacigalupo and his wife Angela. They pointed up the hill from our hotel to Max's villa, the Villino Chiaro. We had found it! Charming and quite modest, with huge tubs of mimosa on the terrace. Massimo (a filmmaker, translator of poetry and essayist) was born in Rapallo and indeed his parent's house was at the centre of Rapallo's cultural life. His father was a friend of Ezra Pound and Massimo himself did a PhD on Pound's post-war Cantos. He is now Professor of American Literature at Genoa University. I enjoyed playing Max. He was erudite and witty and, I feel, had enormous charm.

I think about my career occasionally, I look at the highlights, I look at the lows of which, I have to say there have not been many and certainly no traumatic escapades. Being out of work is something that has not come my way that often. There are many things of which I am proud, and I have been mostly very happy with my performances. Oh yes, one can always do better and the joy of stage work is that one can do better the next night. Of course we are always very dependent on the interaction between the stage and the audience. It's rather like sniffing the air first thing in the morning on a warm day. You know that it is going to be a good experience. But then the real talent, or one of them, is turning an audience, bringing them over to your side, so that the experience is enjoyable for both of you. Acting is, after all, just a job but it is our business to transcend the job.

I am thinking about those many occasions when I have really enjoyed myself and at the apex of those experiences is *Ancestral Voices*. I have to say that this was something that suited me to a T. You will see why.

Ancestral Voices
21 January 2002 I received, out of the blue, a letter from Michael Bloch:
I write, very tentatively, to ask if a certain idea might be of potential interest to you. I am the literary executor of James Lees-Milne (1908-1997) who is particularly known for his wartime diaries, describing his visits on behalf of the National Trust to beleaguered house owners. Hugh Massingberd, the eminent writer, genealogist and obituarist of the Daily Telegraph is keen to adapt the diaries for a one-person show. It's early days and the project may come to nothing, but we were both wondering if the prospect of playing Jim might appeal to you in due course. Hugh cannot think of any living actor who would convey him better. Is this of any interest? Please forgive me for disturbing you: and if so, might I send you a copy of the diaries – if you don't already know them: and might you lunch one day with Hugh and myself?
Yours sincerely
Michael Bloch

So: The three of us met for lunch at the Savile Club near Claridges in Mayfair on 20 February 2002. I had been abstaining from alcohol so ordered an apple juice. They settled for the same. I'm afraid I did most of the talking, partly because, being quite deaf, I find it easier to talk than to listen and partly because I was nervous meeting Hugh for the first time. I trotted out a few of my theatre stories, knowing they were both theatre-goers and they politely laughed in all the right places. It was coming up to 4.30 by the time I found my way to Bond Street underground and home.

I was wondering how long it would take Hugh to write the script. I had previously asked Michael to send me the script and he had replied: "Hugh hasn't written it yet. It's all in his head." Indeed. I invited them both to the Garrick and discovered that Michael had already booked me in to perform in Hugh's club on October 2nd. OK, OK, it is six months ahead, but Hugh has yet to write it and then I have to learn it!! I had written to Hugh and told him not to panic or get stressed. I had heard that he had had a stroke. If needs be, we must postpone the October 2nd date. It transpires that Hugh is writing his memoires which is why he hadn't started on the JL-M script. I, as tactfully as possible, keep making suggestions to him. For instance: the length of the evening. First half forty-five minutes, fifteen minutes for the interval and the second half at thirty-five minutes. I had suggested to Hugh that we play the charming little Jermyn Street theatre and – if he's game – let's go and meet Penny Horner who runs the theatre, after we lunch at Hugh's Club, The Travellers. I told him that in my reading of the diary 1942-1945 James and Stuart were very important in his social life during that time. Hugh said that James Pope-Hennessey was a prominent man in the Literary World and had written a best-selling biography of Queen Mary. Stuart was an American who was lonely in London during the war and found himself swept up into London's society and aesthetic world. Hugh reminded me that James P-H was gay and into 'rough trade' and had had an appalling death in Holland Park. He was beaten up, had a hair-net stuffed down his throat and choked to death. Michael B is just back from New York and says we must meet up soon at the Savile Club for me to meet Charles Hodgson, the Honorary Impresario of the Club.

I have another meeting with Hugh who tells me more about J-L-M – his work, personality, bisexuality and more. We walk from The Travellers Club to see Penny Horner in the Jermyn Street Theatre. The outcome of our meeting is that we are to play Penny's theatre on the 11th November for a week. So Hugh, instead of being a Stage Door Johnnie becomes a West End Producer! Hugh is a lark and I am an owl. He goes to bed at 9 pm and is up at 5.30. He works all the morning and spends his afternoon at Lords in the cricket season. I turn my light out at 2 am and am up again at 9 am. Hugh called to tell me that he has had many offers of support from friends and colleagues: most recently from his friend the artist Julian Barrow who has twice painted James Lees-Milne and will allow us to use one of these paintings for the programme and – if we wish – on fliers or posters.

James Lees-Milne (1908-1997) was firstly an English writer and diarist who in 1936 accepted the position of Country House Secretary at the National Trust. He was alarmed at what he saw in many historic houses – the aftermath of the war, rising costs and severe death duties - and began the work of persuading many owners to pass over their properties to the care of the National Trust to protect them and save them for the nation. His work set in motion the National Trust Act of 1937 which enabled the giving of country houses to the trust free of death duties. He is often regarded as the saviour of our national treasures.

28 June 2002 – an important day…. Michael and I go to meet Hugh who is going to hand over his script. I take it home and find it to be rather scrappy and undramatic and overlong. Not enough tears, not enough laughter. Michael, I'm glad to say, felt much as I did. I read Hugh's script out loud to get an idea of the length. Act I. It took me an hour and thirty-five minutes. I timed it with my grandfather clock. I told Hugh that we must cut at least three-quarters of an hour. In other words, whole chunks must come out, not just a line here and a line there. Nor could we do it by fax, telephone or by letter. We must meet. He agrees to come and see me on the 16th and 17th July at home. And so we persevered and the script came down to a more manageable length. I approached Frith Banbury, who had been a very distinguished West End director, to help me. He was helpful - but would stop me on every line, which both upset and infuriated me. He was then over 80, and I think he was determined to prove he could still direct. On one of my visits to his home he was banging on about my monotone, my singsong delivery, my downward inflection and my sadness. I couldn't believe that only a year or so previously I had been the best Sir Peter Teazle he had ever seen.

Michael Bloch recommended a friend of his called John Bretherton as a possible stage manager. We met and straight away it was apparent he was going to be a real help. He is very intelligent, bright and good company. Well – I did perform as planned at the Savile Club on 2nd October 2002. Hugh had invited many of JL-M's friends to a smart room on the first floor. I had glowing letters from the Chairman of the Savile Club and from Charles Hodgson who wrote "on behalf of all Savilians for a triumphant performance last night." It was the start of some glorious times and Ancestral Voices ran for five years in small theatres and a plethora of wonderful stately homes.

But I cannot leave the beginning of the tale of *Ancestral Voices* without

 paying enormous tribute to two people without whom it would have not been as much fun and whose expertise and knowledge contributed so very much to the success of AV. Take a bow, my stage managers: Christopher Winn who took over from John Bretherton and his wife, Mai Osawa. Christopher, who is the oldest friend of my son-in-law, Rupert, is also the author of the "*I Never Knew That*" series of books which Mai, an author and painter in her own right, illustrates. Between them they handled with peerless aplomb all the technical aspects of the show. We became a little travelling family and in fact Chris and Mai got married during the course of AV's touring.

9

Diary Extracts from the Ancestral Voices tour

FARLEIGH HOUSE: On 21st May, the team lunched with Hugo Vickers and his wife (who is generally called Mouse) in their fine house near Basingstoke. After lunch we drove, with Hugo, to recce Farleigh Wallop and Cumberland Lodge (in Windsor Great Park). The Countess of Portsmouth met us at Farleigh and showed us the fine barn in which we are to play Ancestral Voices. She was most helpful with regard to all our requirements. There are some dodgy-looking unused out-houses and sheds. It looks as though I shall be dressing in one of them….

5 June 2003: Mai and Christopher arrive at my house in Barnes to collect the furniture, props and lighting from my study for the last time. Thank Heavens. From now onwards it will be stored near Ealing for £75 per month. At 1 o'clock the three of us set off to Farleigh House near Basingstoke. We go straight to the barn where we find Annabel (Portsmouth) and her designer friend hanging drapes, setting out chairs and generally making the place most attractive.

The barn is large enough to seat 120 guests at one end of it, have the seating for the performance in the middle and the steps at the end. The stage is excellent: they have brought in rostra and for the first time I won't feel cramped. I will be performing on the most generous stage (15'x21'x3'); wonderful to be able to wander about and be completely unrestricted in all directions.

As for my "dressing room", I am in a huge outhouse which Annabel has carpeted, fixed up a dressing table with a pair of rather grand lights and installed a standard lamp. Some of the entrance has been boarded up with a piece of tarpaulin serving as a door. There is an outside tap where I can wash my hands. The house itself is beautiful; furnished and decorated in the most excellent taste. I have a vast bedroom, 10 yards by 7 yards (vulgar, I know, but I just had to pace it out) and my own bathroom. On my dressing table there are pink pinks and pink roses, picked by Annabel. The bedroom overlooks the front drive and the manicured lawns. Mai and Christopher are in the bedroom next to mine. Another splendid room with two views of the garden; one a long grassed avenue of evergreens, the other another velvet lawn leading to a haha with sheep grazing beyond. There may be a prettier house in England but I don't know of it. Chris, Mai and I dine with Annabel. Quentin Portsmouth does not return from a Conservative meeting until 11.30 so we did not meet him until the following morning at breakfast.

Quentin appears to be one of those people who like to sum you up first (no smile, no attempt to charm) and later melt if he decides to accept you. I would call him an honest and straightforward fellow and I suspect him of being completely trustworthy. He reminded me of a distinguished Spaniard who stayed with us years ago and who talked about the hypocritical good manners of the English. Why smile, he said, and say "how do you do, how lovely to meet you" when there is nothing to smile about and it may turn out not to be "lovely to meet you" after all. Quentin melted later and I liked him. It helped, of course, that he very much enjoyed "*Ancestral Voices*" and said that he had never seen anything like it before. Mind you – there is ambiguity in that statement but I prefer to see the nicer side of it.

After breakfast I went through Act II while Chris and Mai rigged up the lighting and sound in the barn. Hugh arrived in time for lunch after which he went down to the barn for a full rehearsal; partly for me, because we have not done it for 5 week, and partly for Chris and Mai who will be operating the sound and lighting for the first time. I showed Hugh my dressing room before we started. It was just as well because the rain had come in through the roof in a number of places. My dressing table was awash and my act one black shoes were full of water: both shirts and my Act II sweater were damp. Such are the vagaries of ad hoc performance and dressing space. I was given a gas fire which, fully on, dried out the shirts and sweater and, at least externally, the shoes. We were about to start the rehearsal when the lights all went out. Fortunately Annabel was at hand, laying the dinner tables, so she was able to call the right men to find the trip switch or mend the fuse – better to have this problem now than tonight. Chris did ask the fixer whether, if there was a problem during the evening's performance, he could be called on. "No" came the reply "I shall be in Cornwall". Right. Other than that the rehearsal went pretty smoothly. My only reservation was that the lighting was too subtle. In fact too dark. Having played so much comedy over the years I know how essential it is to have lots of light. However, after bringing it all up the three of them assumed there was enough.

The show went pretty well. The audience of 114 were wonderfully quiet and appreciative. I made a short speech at the end, first of all asking the audience to show their appreciation to Hugh for his splendid job in compiling AV, then to thank Quentin and Annabel and Annabel's friend Jocelyn for transforming, most imaginatively, the barn into a theatre. I spoke because it was the launch of our Country House Tour, but I won't do it again. I found it too traumatic following immediately after the final illness of JL-M and his death. I could hardly get the words out. Annabel spoke after me, telling the audience about the charity. The audience had paid £30 for drinks on arrival, the show and the supper. The stage had cost £400 to hire and Annabel thought there would be little left for the charity. At supper Caroline Roe sat on my left. Charming, lived nearby, had three children, her husband commuted to London from Alton. We chatted throughout the first course, but did not have a lot in common. On my right was Anne Scott, elderly, delightful. Must have been beautiful, husband, now deceased, was a Colonel in the Life Guards and Lord Lieutenant of Hampshire – she knew of my brother Johnnie. I spoke to so many people who said they had much enjoyed the evening. Quentin drove me back to the house and suggested a malt whisky night cap. Yes please! Duncan, Annabel's son, and his wife stayed the night. He works for Chatto and Windus and knows Nicky Robinson, James Lees-Milne's nephew. He worked many years ago in Haywood Hill's bookshop and saw JL-M from time to time. He said I had "invaded him and become him". I liked that.

Bed at 1.30 am. Couldn't sleep for thinking about the day and the show and the areas where I could have been better. The following morning after breakfast, C, M and I went for a walk with Annabel and Arthur, her enchanting black and white spaniel. Farleigh House sits in 3-4000 acres. We passed several of the carriage driving obstacles – they have had carriage driving for the past three years. Prince Philip is a keen competitor but now drives a four (rather than a six) carriage. He brings an equerry, a valet and a detective/minder and stays with the Portsmouths in Farleigh House in my (!) bedroom. The next event would be in two weeks.

Quentin is full of surprises. As I said goodbye he not only thanked me for my performance but added that he "would never forget it". C, M and I left at 12.30 having had the most enjoyable time in extreme comfort. Annabel had been a most attentive and generous hostess. Quentin, by the way, told me that he had been very unhappy at Eton. Then, I wondered, why did he send his son there? Did he think his son would be more resilient to the problems he had faced or did he think that times have changed and his son would not have the same problems? I feel that this is a question many parents should ask themselves but I suspect that they bury it deep, deep down to forget the awfulness of their own boarding school days. This is not a universal problem but when it happens it can be devastating and affect you for a good deal of your life.

SOMERSET HOUSE: The Kenneth Clark Lecture Theatre, 9th June 2003 I came on a recce with Hugh about six weeks ago and my heart sank when I saw how shallow the stage was. I like around 14 feet and this was only 8 foot. I asked if the front row of seating could be removed. No – that was out of the question. Covered but not removed. We were there because Maggie Johnson saw AV at the Jermyn Street Theatre and made us an offer. She is a friend of Hugh's so he was keen to agree. He also thought it would look good on our CV! We visited again with Chris and Mai, who could see our problem but they rather looked forward to operating the show from a pukka lighting box behind a glass screen. I dressed in a room that contained over 2000 slides, mostly architectural. No mirror, but a lavatory and basin not far away. Half an hour before the performance one of our lamps blew. When we bought our electrical equipment we had asked for spare bulbs. Not necessary, we were told, "They should last for ever." We had used them for just three performances.

So, knowing that I was playing in a passage rather than on a stage and with one quarter of my lighting missing, I psyched myself up in "the wings" to give the performance of a lifetime! And the customers, about 110 of them, all members of the Royal Society of Literature, were the most attentive and responsive house I have played to. I supped afterwards with Maggie Ferguson and her husband Jamie who is the obituary editor on The Independent. Maggie had been most helpful and solicitous. Lights out at 1.30. I set the alarm for 7 am to catch the 9.30 train from Liverpool Street to Sheringham.

WIVETON HALL: Norfolk 21st June 2003. This is the home, just outside Blakeney, of Desmond and Tina MacCarthy. He is the grandson of the great art critic, Desmond MacCarthy, she is the daughter of Christopher Wakehurst (Lord Wakehurst) and his first wife, Inge, a German designer. The house, dating from the Jacobean era, and garden are equally wild, rambling, shapeless (well – perhaps not the house) but fascinating. Chris, Mai and I are in a long wing. My room overlooks a 10 foot high kitchen garden and a long cottage in which Desmond's mother lives. At mealtimes the table is groaning with superb home or local produce. We had crab on the first night for dinner. Their own honey and honey-comb for breakfast. Polish students are employed to pick raspberries and strawberries in the acres of fields. People come for miles around to "pick your own". Wiveton is rightly famed for its produce and its café.

There are unexpected delights everywhere in the garden. Lots of old-fashioned roses, beds of carnations, marigolds, peonies, sweet williams. Round a corner a little raised area with a lily pond and goldfish. Desmond, who has generous Denis Healey eyebrows, is a most congenial fellow. John and Laura Percival, close family friends, were staying. Laura threw herself into the supper preparations: she is one of those very English young women of a certain type who instinctively know what to do next without having to be told. She teaches art. Nice couple.

I think Desmond realised it might have been wiser for him to have invited 60 people to have come to AV on consecutive nights. Instead of which he invited 120 and was oversubscribed. The room we played in would comfortably have held 70. As it was there were 112 in the main body of the hall and 8 were added to the left of my "stage". Awkward. However – they were all crammed in by 7.45. I started. They were not very responsive. Was it the heat in the airless room? Or the hard seats? Or was it just me not engaging? Chris thought there were too many oldies and oldies don't laugh out loud. But then, afterwards at supper, more people came up to me than ever before, saying how much they had enjoyed themselves. Ah well. There was, though, one old gentleman, wearing an Eton Rambler tie, who did not get on to Jim's wavelength, preferred not to do so. For him, Jim came into the category of men who discover their sexual direction and should shoot themselves. The new head of the National Trust, Sir William Proby, was there. He thanked me for my letter. I had completely forgotten that I had written to him and asked him what on earth I had said. He replied that I must have written telling him about AV. Later I remembered congratulating him on his appointment. Had he forgotten that too?

The following morning Desmond showed us a barn made of timbers, brick and stone, which he is endeavouring to turn into a performance space. He has already rescued the roof to the tune of £15,000. I was able to advise him a little on the stage, acoustics, electric points and dressing rooms. It would, indeed, make a little theatre. It even has a little raised area above and behind the stage where a small orchestra could play for touring opera.

Let's hope he can get a 50% grant towards further conversion.

Chris and Mai drove me to Sheringham Station to catch the 11.56 to Norwich and thence to Liverpool Street. They went on to look at Blickling Hall. All in all a fascinating visit but we missed Hugh dreadfully. He had left at tea-time to join his daughter's birthday celebrations in London. It is the only performance he has missed since we opened at the Savile Club on 2nd October last year.

PETWORTH HOUSE: Recce 23rd May and Performance 9 July 2003 Hugh and I caught a midmorning train from Victoria to Pulborough in West Sussex. We were met by the charming and efficient (her last job was at Balmoral) secretary of Lord Egremont, Miss Mearns. We are greeted most warmly at Petworth House by Max and Caroline Egremont. This is a sentimental journey for me. In my prep school days, my family had moved from London into a little cottage two miles from Petworth on the Kirdford Road. My father created a wonderful garden and we enjoyed many holidays there leading up to the Second World War.

We saw quite a lot of Charles and Violet Leconfield and their two adopted children, Elizabeth and Peter. They were not blood siblings and it was patently obvious to us that Elizabeth fitted in to the grandeur of Petworth House most happily. Not so Peter. He did not, for instance, enjoy the hunting. Once, when we were all out cub hunting, the Watsons all on foot, Peter trotted up to me in a copse and asked me if I would like a ride on his lint white pony. I told him what he already knew, that his father, a frightening presence to small boys, would not be best pleased to see his son on foot and me mounted on his pony. Peter did not fit in to the aristocratic life. After he left Eton, he refused to go into the Guards. Instead he went into the Royal Sussex Regiment but would not take a commission. He married and had a son, but, in his middle years, took his own life. It's a little nugget of sadness that remains with me.

My brothers and I often bicycled over to Petworth House. We raced round the basement and in the kitchen garden. I had a soft spot for Fred Streeter, the head gardener. We shared a birthday. He used to yell at us, though, if we rode over his grass edges. Fred became the first radio gardener with his famous catch phrase "the answer lies in the soil" – which was taken up by Kenneth Williams in *Round the Horne*. For years Fred would send a hamper of fruit and vegetable up to "Master Peter" in London in the spring and summer. His family ran the jewellers shop on the corner of Lombard Street opposite the church. He was over 100 years when he died. We never saw much of Lordy; he seemed to spend most of his day in his study but Violet was much in evidence and was very good to my mother when our father was killed in Belgium a week before Dunkirk.

After Hugh and I arrived at the house, Max Egremont threw his arms wide and said "I thought we'd have you show in here". We were in the White Library. Hugh and I looked at each other. We knew immediately that it was too small *and* the wrong shape. We looked at several other rooms, nearly plumped for the marble drawing Room but eventually settled for the Oblong Dining Room – though I was unhappy, being a superstitious actor – by a vast oil painting depicting a scene from Shakespeare's Scottish play. See – I can't bring myself to mention it even here. Obviously, I would just have to rise above it. After a delicious lunch – Dover sole and asparagus, strawberries and meringues – Miss Mearns drove us back to Pulborough Station to catch the 3.02 back to London. A good day.

I found it most moving to be back in Petworth and Petworth House after so many years. My first impression is that the garden is glorious. Caroline Egremont is a keen gardener and has done wonders with the garden. It is unrecognizable from the gardens I remember before the 2nd World War. I have a splendid room, which doubles as my dressing room for *"Ancestral Voices"*, looking straight towards the church. The sun pours through the windows in the morning. There is a beautiful pot plant and sweet peas on the dressing table – in fact there are flowers in pots or vases all over the house: geraniums, lilies and orchids. While Chris and Mai were setting up the stage, furniture and lighting in the morning I took myself off to the garden and swimming pool area to go through the entire script out loud on my own. I felt this necessary because it had been three weeks since my last performance. At 12.30 Caroline appeared with one of the golden retrievers. I had just finished the second act and we had a swim. It was wonderfully sunny and the water was warm. After lunch we had the usual topping and tailing rehearsal. At 7 o'clock I heard the first guests arriving. They were to have a meal first and I was called down at 9. It was a full house of ninety-nine; each paying £45 each with all profits going to the Cottage Hospital.

Hugh had found a short piece for me to insert for the occasion. JLM had visited Lord (Charles) Leconfield who did show him the house but was sceptical about the National Trust scheme and did not give Jim a very warm welcome. At the end of the afternoon he bade him goodbye while pointing to the tea house over the road adding "I understand they do very good snacks over there – put yours down to me." Jim looked at the tea house (this was the Four and Twenty Blackbirds of pre-war fame) and saw a notice hanging in the window stating "Closed".

My brother Johnnie and his wife Lavinia were in the audience. I went down to find them after the show but they had already left. It was well after 11 and they usually go to bed at 9. So very different from the owl life of the actor! Michael Bloch (JLM's literary editor) was with John Bretherton and Paul Lund. I spoke to Andrew (AN) Wilson and several Wyndham relations of the Egremonts who seemed to have enjoyed themselves. Hugh, Chris, Mai and I had a jolly supper in the kitchen after George Wyndham (son of the Egremonts) found a large scotch and soda for me. George is splendidly modern young man of 20: tattoo on his stomach, ring in an eyebrow and jeans with drooping crotch down to his knees. Very fashionable. The old Lord Leconfield – Lordy – that I had known 65 years or so previously would have had a fit. Caroline showed us Turner's studio, a vast and truly handsome room containing his easel and a hundred or so old leather bound books. There are 21 Turners in the house. Hugh and I went into the church which was much gloomier than I remembered as a small boy in the late thirties. There has been, I understand, much talk about putting a spire on the church as was there when Turner was working at Petworth House and indeed when my family lived nearby, but alas, no inked-in plans.

For me this was the most nostalgic night of the entire country house tour. Having so many vivid memories of Petworth and Petworth House when I was nine years old, now to be playing in one of the great rooms there 65 years later was surprisingly emotional. My memories include Lord and Lady Leconfield (Charles and Violet), their adopted children Elizabeth and Peter, Fred Streeter the head gardener, Colonel and Mrs Maitland who ran the Four and Twenty Blackbirds Restaurant opposite the church, the Briggs family (Captain Briggs worked for Lord Leconfield), bicycling in the kitchen garden and in the basement of the House, the bombing of the school, and my father - although a territorial in the Middlesex Yeomanry - joining up in the Royal Sussex Regiment and being killed in Belgium on May 21 1940.

CHESWORTH: 12 July 2003. Ever since Hugh and I visited Chesworth in Horsham on a recce we have been looking forward to playing the little chapel adjoining the house. Anyone that I mention Chesworth to says "where's that?". The reason they do not know it is because it is privately owned and has never been opened to the public. Eben and Themy

Hamilton bought it from Laurence Evans, a most distinguished actors' agent, who had lived there for some 40 years. The Hamiltons have been there for 10. When Laurence Evans bought it he must have locked up the little chapel and kept it locked during his tenure. The Hamiltons, however, have not only opened it up and restored all the brickwork, but now have musical evenings and performances such as ours. They have also, incidentally, transformed the garden which had become quite wild into something most magical. There are waterways, waterfalls, lakes and ponds. Themy has a young gardener, Kevin, who is full time. She takes him to nurseries and open gardens; they are, obviously, a great team. Eben is a lawyer of some distinction, spending much of his time in Hong Kong. A most handsome man, about 6'4", thick wavy hair. A fine host – as indeed, Themy, who is Indian, is a fine hostess. Our team all stayed in the house and we could not have been more comfortable. The chapel holds 73 people. They were not charged but were told that proceeds from the event would go to Chailey Heritage for Children who, from birth, are mentally and physically disabled. This charity, incidentally, was started by a woman called Betty Kimmins. Her daughter, Verena Hanbury became a great friend of mine when she was stage managing on *The Grass Is Greener*, at The St. Martin's Theatre. Verena's daughter, Lucinda, is now my God Daughter.

The stage was a little smaller than I like. I was not able to roam around the area as I would usually do and added to this there was a spongy feeling underfoot. In certain places I was obliged to lean on the furniture for safety. I got used to it but it was not a little like trampolining. It was one of the hottest nights of the year. The audience arrived at about 7.30 and enjoyed their drinks on the lawn and in the gardens around the house. They had a full sit down dinner at 8 and AV at 9. I rather felt the lack of lighting, often just one spotlight on me, caused a lack of laughter and told Hugh so in the interval. But there was much applause at the end and I spoke to many of the audience afterwards who, genuinely, seemed to have enjoyed the evening. When I heard at breakfast that they had consumed 76 bottles of champagne I was amazed they were neither rowdy nor asleep during the performance.

The evening was a considerable success due to the enthusiasm and energy of the hosts and later I received a letter from Themy saying they had raised £2,320 for Chailey Heritage. My old friend, Verena Hanbury, who was there with her husband Ben, is head of the Chailey Heritage and must have been enormously pleased with that result. We would never have been at

Chesworth if it had not been for Larry Dalzell, the theatrical agent who is a friend of the Hamiltons and who recommended AV to them. He would have been there but sadly our visit coincided with an operation on his knee and he was unable to make it. Were we never to go to another venue after Chesworth our memories of the Hamiltons and the house are so treasured that we would be happy ever after. We have become good friends.

SLEDMERE HOUSE: 16th August 2003. Kings Cross to Malton via York with Hugh. Chris met us. I have another huge bedroom, with a four poster bed. We are to do the show in the most glorious library. In fact it was this library at Sledmere that first set Hugh thinking about our doing a tour of country houses. Sir Tatton Sykes, our host, has had a perfect stage built by his estate workers to the exact dimension that we like; 18x15x2 ft. My bedroom looks onto a beautiful formal garden with curling box hedges, shaped as an S for Sykes, masses of white, pink and mauve petunias. Beyond is the church, great lawns and a fountain, rose beds with La Perle D'Azure – a particularly beautiful clematis - outside a vast walled garden.

As there is no entrance or exit directly off the stage, Tatton has lent us a fine four panel screen which is in the top right hand corner. I will appear from behind it for the commencement of Act I and use it for the exits for both acts. We have also borrowed some small library steps to dress the stage up right. In fact we are so keen on the screen that we want to try and buy one and use it for all future venues where there is no handy and convenient exit.

Tatton has a house party for the event. Hugh and I are in the house. Chris and Mai are round the corner in the pub, but mostly eat with us in Sledmere House. We are given delicious meals cooked by Maureen (spectacular summer pudding, vanilla ice cream, a particularly delicious bread and butter pudding) and served most efficiently by charming middle-aged ladies wearing white gloves. On the day of the event I disappear to my bedroom to go through all the words, doze off a little and have a bath. Most of the guests swam. At 7.20 Hugh took me down to my chair behind the screen. Then the audience, 99 of them, came in and we started on time at 7.30.

I always give a slightly different performance depending on how and where the audience are placed. In the Sledmere library they are seated on comfortable chairs but in spite of that I felt they were too formal in their placing. Eight inches between each chair. During the day I had moved them all closer together but still I felt my performance was a little more formal than I like. A contrast to a performance in the Pavilion at Thorpe Tilney where they were almost on top of me on three sides: the laughter there was certainly more pronounced. I do not mean to say that the audience, black ties and evening dress, at Sledmere did not enjoy themselves, at least I hope so. They all stayed on for a buffet supper. My friend Andrew McDonnell (focus puller on the Darling Buds of May, now a cameraman on Born and Bred) and his girlfriend, Kim (who had worked with my son-in-law, Rupert, on Heartbeat) drove over from Guiseley. Also there were Nigel and Malize Forbes-Adams with one of his sons, Pip. Tatton's brother, Jeremy, gave me a long, strong scotch. Wonderful. I am always anxious for the performance to be well received, of course, but particularly so when the host has gone to great lengths to try and ensure that not only the show is a success but the whole weekend. Here, at Sledmere, Tatton had had the stage built, arranged for black drapes to be hung on windows (so we could start with a blackout) and in every way fulfilled our every wish. He filled the house with some of his closest friends and had obviously discussed every minor detail with Mrs Hines, his right hand lady, to ensure everything went smoothly.

After lunch on Sunday Tatton drove Michael Crawcour and me to York to catch a train back to London. Tatton will certainly go down in the annals of Sledmere with considerable credit for what he has contributed and achieved; many pictures, some exciting interior decoration and now he is embarking on a huge orangery beyond the dining room as well as many innovations in the gardens.

THE ROYAL GEOGRAPHICAL SOCIETY: 31st October 2003. Charity performances for two Indian charities. It is so pleasing for us to know that a considerable percentage of the money made from our performances of *Ancestral Voices* goes to charity.

A few years ago I took part in a performance at Harewood House for Helen Taylor Thompson and her Starfish charity. I suggested giving a performance of *Ancestral Voices* for her and she leaped at the idea. Within months we were playing The Royal Geographical Society (next door to the Albert Hall) for two Indian Charities: Thare Machi (Helen's Starfish Initiative) and Jaisalmer in Jeopardy. Jaisalmer is a 12th century fort in the Thar desert of Rajasthan. It is of unique historic interest and is on the verge of collapse.

The RGS main space is essentially a lecture theatre. When the team made a recce there we were doubtful if it would be suitable for us. The stage area was simply not deep enough – about nine foot instead of the fourteen we ideally need. On the platform there is a lectern and microphone. However, Nicholas Leevers, the RGS Events co-ordinator, thought it might be possible to add an 'apron' to the stage. It was put out to tender and quotes came in of £850 and £1000. This was out of the question if worthwhile cheques were to be given to the charities. Then one of Helen's team, Stephen Clarke, offered to construct an apron stage himself. Cost of timber: £150, labour: nil. And a superb job he did. Stephen calculated that it could take 18 stone at any one time.

As it is a one man show and I am 12 stone – no problem! There was a period of about 2 weeks before the event when, because the box office was so quiet, the RGS were considering putting us in one of their rooms instead of the lecture theatre. The room would seat 120. Happily there were some late bookings and we played to over 200 in the main house. Julie Ronald, PR for the RGS, was truly supportive throughout and determined that the evening should be a success. My brother Michael came for the second time. Michael Bloch came for the umpteenth time and brought a party of nine including Michael Strassen, the singer who is helping us with our plans to make a video of *Ancestral Voices*.

ARCHERS HALL, EDINBURGH: 1-3 Dec 2003. The Queen's Body Guard for Scotland, the royal Company of Archers was founded in 1676. We are playing in the grand room on the first floor where there are many fine portraits of previous Captains-General on the walls and there is an excellent Raeburn beside my stage of Dr Nathaniel Spens of Craingsanquhar painted in the Archer's stance.

The three performances we are doing here have been arranged by my friend Martin Haldane of Gleneagles. He had considered having us in the Innerpeffray Library but decided it was too small. Hugh and I are staying with Martin and his wife Petronella. We generally go up at 7.30 but the first night was delayed until 7.45 because my old school friend, James Cayzer, who was coming from Kinpurnie Castle in Angus, had difficulty in finding the Hall. The acoustics are tricky. Most people heard all right but Hugh thought it might be advisable to pitch it even harder and more slowly for the next two performances. My godson, Philip Dundas, was at the second performance as was Mary Strathmore. It was the first anniversary of AV and the 50th performance and Hugh arranged for Mai to present me with a magnificent bunch of flowers. Very kind and very typical of him. Martin made a brief speech.

After the show Hugh treated the team, Martin, Petronella and Philip to a dinner at the Fisher restaurant. Superb lobster.

On the second day the team drove to Leith. We looked over the Royal Yacht

Britannia in her final berth – very enjoyable – then lunched at the Waterfront Wine Bar and Bistro. We all lamented on the sad fact that the Queen no longer has a Royal Yacht and we all felt that, in spite of its expense, it was one of the more necessary perks of a monarch when showing off her country. We are where we are but I still have to say it is a pity and a loss to the country.

I have never before delivered the play as I did at the third performance. Pitched strongly with extra clear diction – it was also my most accurate rendering. But this did not help the show comedically. Inevitably I lost the intimacy and the fun of the throw-away lines. In other words the laughter was much subdued. I knew, though, that I had to play this way: the acoustics were so poor, most of the audience were retired and many had a hearing problem. Mary Strathmore did not like me, in my character of JL-M, referring to the Queen Mother's "sugary insincerity". She said, and she should know, "It simply wasn't true. People did not know her. It is derogatory and unkind." We may cut it anyway. These three performances were the only ones to date in Scotland but we hope to return next year, perhaps to play at Glamis Castle and, possibly, the Festival.

DODDINGTON PLACE: October 2003. A letter from Amicia Oldfield:
Dear Hugh,
We simply adored putting on Ancestral Voices. Thank you and your charming entourage very much for making it such a success. The hall was the perfect setting. I've always wondered whether it would lend itself to events and this has proved it does. It was so exciting preparing for it, clearing the hall, watching the stage go up. I just wish in some ways I had been a guest coming to the event. One can never tell what an event is like from the outside! But judging by the thank you letters we have had, everyone else was just as enthusiastic as Richard and myself. Let me know when I can see AV again. I could easily become a groupie!
Lots of love, Amicia.

This particular performance raised a brilliant £5,280. Doddington Place is owned by Richard and Amicia Oldfield, in whose family it has been since 1906. The gardens are recognised by English Heritage as being of special historical interest. They extend to over ten acres with a woodland garden (azaleas, rhododendrons), a Spring garden, a sunken garden, an Edwardian rock garden and most particularly, and famously, the unfettered yew hedge. This used to be clipped into geometrical neatness but when war broke out in 1939 it was left to grow untended and is now clipped only once a year to keep its cloudy billows. The yew clippings are sent to a pharmaceutical firm for processing as part of a cancer treatment drug. The house itself was built in 1860 in the Victorian Tudor style, not perhaps my favourite style, but pretty impressive nevertheless. And we were VERY well looked after.

CHATSWORTH: The Duke of Devonshire died in 2004, on 3 May. I was booked to play at Chatsworth on 21 May 2004 and we did wonder, Hugh and I, if the performance would be cancelled or postponed. But the majority of the people we spoke to in the days running up to the event considered cancellation or postponement unlikely because a) the Duchess was very much a life-must-go-on sort of person and b) she had a large staff who were most capable of looking after us.

James Lees-Milne and Deborah Devonshire were close friends. He often stayed at Chatsworth. Indeed, after his wife, Alvilde, died, he always went to Chatsworth for Christmas. So, because of their close friendship the Duke was keen to arrange a performance of *Ancestral Voices* for Debo especially as, because of ill health, they had not been able to come to a performance at the Jermyn Street theatre where for one evening they had booked every seat.

My only previous visit to Chatsworth had been many years ago when I was appearing in the Buxton festival. On that occasion I was only able to see the garden, so I was excited to be back. Condolence cards has been pouring in to the Duchess; so much so that she suggested that the staff display them throughout the house on grand pianos, shelves, mantelpieces and chests of drawers; as many flat surfaces as there were able to be covered. By the time of the performance she had received six hundred and fifty cards. And they were still arriving. It was very moving.

It was Hugh's habit to discover something personal in the Diaries about each owner of the houses in which we performed and he duly found a charming description of the Duke which I added to my performance and also a piece about Lismore Castle, their home in Ireland.

The performance to about 70 was in their private dining room. My dressing room was the servants' sitting room. When I was dressed and ready to start at 7.25, I wandered into the kitchen, which adjoined the sitting room. The young chef was whipping up a hollandaise sauce. He was preparing the Duchess's dinner: soup, asparagus and scrambled eggs. She was not going to be joining the audience – she was staying in her room. Henry, the butler, who had been at Chatsworth for 41 years, was standing by to take it up to the Duchess. I went "on stage" at 7.30, just as Henry disappeared upstairs with the tray. All the staff seemed to be devoted and dedicated to the Devonshires and Chatsworth. Not least among them was Helen Marchant who looked after the "AV" team. Helen had been their private secretary for 18 years. As well as dealing with the busy mail pouring in daily, she is helping the Duchess to organise the memorial services for the Duke. One locally, one near their Irish castle and one in the Guards Chapel in London. Before we left, Helen told me that many of the workers on the estate who had attended my performance were openly weeping at the references to the Devonshires; the Duke having so recently died and the Duchess, whom we never actually saw, grieving in the room above us. It was a good mixture of punters, young and old, jeans and dinner jackets. As is often the case, much of the laughter came from the back. Those in the front, silver haired, upright, walking sticks, hearing aids and soundless laughter. Hugh told me afterwards that one of the posh elderlies told him that we should cut the dog dying section: "Far too upsetting for an audience" apparently. Chatsworth was our 75th performance.

CLIVEDEN 2004: I have to say that Cliveden is not the sort of hotel that I usually stay at! The ratio of guests to staff is three to one! Cliveden, as everyone must remember, was the scene of the various interactions and exchanges between the then Secretary of State for War, Jack Profumo, the osteopath Stephen Ward and the two girls, Christine Keeler and Mandy Rice–Davies. That whole 1960s scandal has been so much written about and examined I am not going to do any of that here. Suffice to say that Cliveden is both glamorous and luxurious par excellence.

It has had something of a chequered history. The original house, built in 1666 by the second Duke of Buckingham, was destroyed by fire in 1795 and left derelict. Sir George Warrender, who was an MP between 1807-1832, and who was dubbed Sir George Provender by Sidney Smith because of his propensity for good living, bought it from Lady Orkney's grandson in 1824 and commissioned William Burn to rebuild the main block. It burned down again in 1849. Each time it has been rebuilt into a house more stunning than the previous one.

It has been home and host to some of England's more notorious characters and a political and social hub particularly during the middle years of the twentieth century. When it first became the luxurious country house hotel it now is, electric gates were installed at the end of the drive. They opened all right, but closed far too quickly. Result? Crushed Bentleys and Rolls Royces. The gates were dismantled.

The visit to Cliveden came about because I had run into Chris Luscombe (actor and director) at the naming ceremony for the ship, Minerva II, in the Pool of London. He had heard about *Ancestral Voices* and was keen to book it for the Cliveden Club Members. He asked me how long the show lasted. I said that it was two hours with a twenty minute interval. "Can you cut it down to 50 minutes without an interval?" "No, I can't. But if you like I'll just do Act I which lasts for 50 minutes. If you provide the programme they need not know about Act II. Act I is quite formidable in itself."

The Cliveden Club Members pay around £2500 per annum for the use of the Hotel and all its facilities. For this they also get a 50 minute entertainment once a month on Sunday evenings throughout the winter, followed by a black tie dinner after the performance. Hugh came with us as usual. So, with Chris, Mai and my son Robin, who came to help with the lighting and who drove me down to Taplow, we were five. We were all to arrive in the afternoon of the performance and stay on for lunch the following day. Our room was wonderfully luxurious. En-suite with bathroom of course. Little five star extras like a long shoe horn, a clothes brush, champagne in an ice bucket, two glasses. An orchid. Lovely. My show was to be in the Grand Hall just inside the main entrance. There was not to be any platform or stage but they provided me with a lectern instead of my usual desk and high chair. It worked quite well but I did have to concentrate like mad for the first ten minutes or so as hotel guests were arriving behind the audience and there were a dozen staff milling about – all as if I didn't exist.

There were about forty in the audience, seated on sofas and arm chairs, many with drinks. They were most sympathetic. It was just like playing to friends in a drawing room; not least because Chris Luscombe had invited my daughter Emma and her husband Rupert to the event. It was wonderful to have them there. Next morning the team had decided to meet in the Hall at 8.30 to swim in the two heated pools - one outside and one inside. Wonderful. Before lunch the five of us went for a walk and then we were driven in one of the hotel vehicles to Spring Cottage. Very attractive with two double bedrooms, dining room and kitchen – plus butler provided. It makes an idyllic place to spend a weekend, or more. Spring Cottage had been rented by the notorious Stephen Ward (back to the Profumo Affair) which somehow lends the cottage an air of raffish history. Cliveden was a terrific experience for all of us. Many thanks to Sarah Ducker at Cliveden and to Chris Luscombe for suggesting us to her.

Andrew Lloyd Weber wrote a musical called *Stephen Ward* based on the whole Profumo story. When I went to a matinee the theatre was packed with white haired old ladies, and me, who had heard of Dr Ward and remembered all the scandal. But I am afraid that the young were not so interested. I don't know whether the story is just not relevant these days or whether it was the medium of a musical. I think that the Profumo affair does remain interesting because of the personalities involved, for the frailty and weakness of human nature and for the things one does for lust, as it were.

GLAMIS CASTLE: 26 April, 2004. Taken from my diary. My visit to Glamis. The Earl of Strathmore's father, Fergus Bowes-Lyon who became the 17th Earl, was a friend of mine at Eton. Isobel, the current countess, welcomes us most warmly. She is as unstuffy as a countess could be and has a wonderfully infectious, idiosyncratic laugh. She showed me to my bedroom and told me Princess Margaret was born in it. My dressing room for the performance is the sitting room which was always used by the Queen Mother when she came to stay.

We are playing AV in the Drawing Room; a magnificent room indeed. Family portraits everywhere and two Van Dycks – Elizabeth 1st and Charles 1st. The staging that they have hired is not really large enough but just serviceable. The seating, those all-in-one Bakelite chairs with two vast sofas in the front row. My old school friend James Cayzer sat on one of the sofas. I heard after the performance that he went off to sleep soon after I began and snored. I never saw him as the audience were hardly lit at all and being half deaf I never heard him. James now looks more like Nigel Bruce (Watson in the early Sherlock Holmes films) than Nigel Bruce himself.

Isobel looks after us very well. The cooking is superb, including the breakfast of porridge and mixed grill. The cook, Ray, looks uncannily like Anthony Hopkins. My first impression was that Hopkins, that multi-talented creature, was moonlighting.

The morning after the show, I move out of the castle and stay nearby in Glamis House

From L: Me, Eden Vansittart, Mary, Dowager Countess of Strathmore, Loelia Vansittart, Rupert Vansittart, Hugh Massingberd, Christopher Winn, Mai Winn with Mary Strathmore, Fergus' widow. She lives in what used to be the factor's house. It had one bedroom when Mary decided to live in it. It now has five bedrooms and five bathrooms. A most attractive 'des res' with a well tended garden. Mary had made one of the bedrooms into a nursery. It is all ready to pass on but not, I hope, for many years; she is only 72. My daughter Emma and her family were staying nearby so they came to Glamis for the day. Mary kindly gave us lunch in the restaurant and a conducted tour of the castle. It was a beautiful day and we all enjoyed ourselves immensely. That evening before retiring I took Mary out to dinner to a restaurant of her choosing, The Park Tavern run by a young man, known to many, called Tim Duncan, who, alas, was out for the evening.

ELLEN TERRY'S BARN: Small Hythe, Kent, 8 September 2004. The team are very happy to be back in Kent, particularly as Richard and Amicia Oldfield have very kindly invited us to stay at Doddington Place for four nights. Their home will be our base while we give performances first in Ellen Terry's barn in Smallhythe Place, just outside Tenterden, and then at a barn in the grounds of Goodnestone Park for Brook and Margaret Fitzwalter.

We arrive at Doddington. The eldest son is wandering round the huge garden waiting to be taken back to Eton for the Autumn term. The middle one has already left for his prep school and the youngest, Edward, is reluctant to go to bed! Their older sister, Leonora, is on her gap year before going to Leeds University to read English.

The team had made a recce of Smallhythe back on 8th July. We had found the barn closed: they were undergoing a complete overhaul.   The auditorium was a giant sand pit. Workmen everywhere. The transformation is marvellous. It is now in working order, without losing any of its magical character and atmosphere, and is the perfect space for AV. There's a new lighting board and equipment, comfortable seating for 75, spacious dressing room into which some thoughtful person had placed three large vases of herbaceous flowers from the garden. To the left of my make-up table there is a life-size terracotta bust of Ellen Terry as Portia, her kind eyes staring at me. I feel that she is wishing me well as I prepare for my performance.

The auguries are good. Sybil Thorndike's nephew, Daniel,with whom I appeared in *The Doctor's Dilemma* at the Haymarket in London in 1963, made a short speech before our play because tonight was the 75th anniversary of the opening of the barn as a theatre by Edith Craig – Ellen Terry's daughter. I spoke after the play, which I never normally do. I first of all thanked them for being so appreciative which they, assuredly, had been. I then told them how pleased I was to be back on the stage where I had given my first professional performance in July 1950. Then I read out an excerpt from a card I had received, only yesterday, from my good friend, Wendy Toye. "So lovely for you to be back in Ellen Terry's barn. Did I ever tell you that I was in Ellen Terry's last performance of *The Crossings at the Lyric*, Hammersmith? I was about 6 years old, I think. I had to guide her on, because she was nearly blind and I had to squeeze her hand when it was her turn to speak, because she was very deaf and could not hear her cues. I was chosen out of all the children, including Angela Baddeley, to do this. I was so proud. She was in a huge chair and I sat on a tiny stool by her feet."

We thanked Susannah, our hostess, for having us and managed to get away by 10.30. Hugh took the team to an excellent Turkish restaurant called Ösgür in Tenterden. The Turk who owns it is called Mehmet Özel – or George!. Virginia Ironside, AN Wilson and his wife Ruth are staying for the weekend with the Oldfields. Also Giles Wood, the artist and his wife Mary Killen, the journalist. As well as having nine people staying in the house, the Oldfields calmly and, seemingly effortlessly have a lunch party for 15 on the Sunday. Amazing, generous people. And both so handsome. It's not fair…

HOUGHTON HALL: near King's Lynn, Norfolk. 18 September 2004. When I told my friend, Michael Crawcour, that I was going to play *Ancestral Voices* in Houghton Hall, he said "You are a lucky man. Houghton is the prettiest house in England and David Cholmondeley is the nicest of men." And so it turned out. The performance is in aid of the CPRE, the Council for the Protection of Rural England. David, who is in his early 40's is the most excellent host. He looks over ones shoulder occasionally, not, I hope, to see if he is missing out on someone more exciting and interesting, but just to make sure that his other guests are not out on a limb or drink-less. All his guests seem to have driven up from London, all seeing AV and staying the night. Meals are served by white bloused ladies and a butler.

As so often before, I have a wonderfully spacious bedroom, with bathroom en-suite (equipped with a virgin toothbrush, toothpaste, and razor and shaving soap), overlooking parkland with hundreds of white deer. Medieval and ghostly and very arresting. Straight ahead, about 100 yards away, is what looks to me like a huge circular piece of plastic. I assume this is marking the area where David is going to place a fountain, or a statue, or whatever. How wrong can one be! On Sunday, before our departure, he and his two white Labradors, so in keeping with the white deer, give us a conducted tour of the garden which he has transformed. That piece of plastic, on closer inspection, indeed turns out to be a sculpture. Nowhere is it higher than two foot and consists of hundreds of chunks of deep slate leaning against each other. David says "It grows on you."

Michael Bloch and John Bratherton, after an awful drive up from London, saw AV and stayed the weekend with Dominic Harrod, for many years the BBC's Economics Editor, who lives nearby.

And finally

HATFIELD HOUSE: 15 December 2006 From The Marquess of Salisbury, Chelsea, London. Typed 9 March 2006

Dear Mr Watson

Thank you for your nice letter of the 3rd March. Jonathan (Cecil) spoke of you with great affection when he and Anna came to stay with us the other day. There was, at one moment, a possibility that you might bring 'Ancestral Voices' to Cranborne. Sadly, we had to decline the honour, because the house really wasn't big enough to accommodate what you needed. It would be the greatest possible fun, were you to come to Hatfield. However, I really must consult my wife, who is the dominating force in our household., I know she would welcome it in principle. Would the easiest thing be for you perhaps, had you a second, to come here for a drink one evening to discuss the matter with us both?

Yours sincerely

Robert

So to Hatfield we go on 15th December. Hugh writes me two pieces about Hatfield House. The first into Act I:

On a visit to Oxford I find myself sitting next to David Cecil after dinner at Christ Church. It is difficult to reconcile his Dresden china appearance with his ever accelerating loquacity, twinkling of eyes, twisting of long fingers and loose-limbed jerkiness. Rather disconcerting. I felt like a slow-witted bull beside him. He talked of Hatfield when he was a child; of the terrifying intellectual level of the conversation, and the devotional atmosphere. I imagine there was something a bit forced about both. I remember David's nephew Andrew Cavendish telling me that Hatfield was much larger than Chatsworth and the Salisburys much richer!

 The second to go into Act II:

I remember that it was in the summer of 1948 that I first saw one of my favourite places, Cranborne, the secondary seat of the Marquesses of Salisbury, a dear, romantic, isolated manor house in Dorset.   What a dream! The green ride heading through iron gates to a rise of ground, most effective. Enticing meadows beyond, as though promising a world of the spirit somewhere out of sight. The garden simple and sweet with orchard trees amongst herbaceous borders. Lord Salisbury, who had succeeded as the 5th Marquess the previous year, was most friendly.

12 May 2006
My dear Moray
*Herewith, as promised, a couple of suggested **inserts** for your **Hatfield** performance of Ancestral Voices later in the year. As I'm sure you know, Cecil should be pronounced 'Sissel' and Cranborne 'Cranb'n. Do hope you're flourishing, and that your Jersey adventure goes swimmingly. Best love as ever Hugh.*

Well – it went well! The letter, handwritten, from Robert says it all:

18 December 2006
Dear Moray
I hope you know how much pleasure you gave to one and all on Friday evening. We all thought the evening a triumph with the subtleties of your performance coming back to haunt and amuse throughout the weekend. The audience loved every moment and there are already calls for a repeat. I do hope you were not too exhausted by it all, what with the performance and the revelry in the kitchen afterwards. However we all loved it. Thank you a million times for giving us all such pleasure. Yours ever, Robert.

Couldn't have put it better meself!

10

Family and Barnes

My Wife, Pam

Pam was born on Long Island, New York, in 1923. Her parents, Dorothy and Percy Marmont were English, but had been staying for a week in New York when the director, Ben Iden-Payne spotted Percy strolling down Fith Avenue and talked him into being in his latest production on Broadway. This led the family on to Hollywood, where Percy had a marvellous career as a silent film star. Then, in 1927, they returned to live in England.

During the war Pam and her sister, Patricia, went from being Land Girls, to Wrens, to the American Army. They were stationed in Bavaria where Pam sang for the troops. Later on, in Versailles, she also sang in a troupe of US Army entertainers that included Mickey Rooney! Then she and I were in the same year at The Webber Douglas Drama Academy of Singing and Dramatic Art. Pam left early to play Giggling Gertie in *Oklahoma* at The Drury Lane Theatre and to understudy Ado Annie. She then went on to tour in *Treasure Hunt* with Sybil Thorndike and Hugh Casson and then on to the very successful Lyric and Globe Reviews with Dora Bryan, Ian Carmichael and Joan Heal. Joan's nephew, Rupert Vansittart, as yet unborn, many years later would become my son-in-law!

Our wedding, on 28th June 1955, took place in the Chancel of Chelsea Old Church, as the main part of the church had not yet been restored after being bombed in The Second World War. Pam looked wonderful. She had made her own dress of white lace and carried a bouquet of yellow roses. Maude Carpenter came from her home in The Wirral, leaving at 6.00am telling The Morning Post, "This was one function I couldn't miss!" Maude and Percy had worked together at The Liverpool Playhouse in 1916.

After a week's Honeymoon in Kent (penniless actors remember!) Pam and I did *Small Hotel* together with Gordon Harker (great-uncle to Susanna and Caroline) and Marjorie Fielding, at the St. Martin's Theatre. Two years later Emma, our daughter, was born, and then two years after that our son Robin.

Pam took to being a fulltime mother, aged thirty four, with much devotion. Twenty years later she found a whole new career as a local councillor in Sussex.

She was a superbly inventive cook and hostess, managing to make our home always full of warmth and comfort. Luckily she enjoyed our return back to London saying she had more fun meeting up with old friends at the actor's church, St. Paul's, for memorial services than going to the theatre! Tragically, in 1999, aged seventy six, Pam died very suddenly of CJD (Creutzfeld-Jakob Disease). She faced this horror with immense dignity and humour. Her dear cousins David and Angelina came over from Spain helping us all with the painful hospital visits.

She remembered once, her father, Percy telling her, "It's your role to keep us all entertained!" She certainly took this to heart. Her brilliant, creative spirit lives on in our lives today.

Emma, my daughter

I was on tour with *The Grass Is Greener* in Aberdeen, in 1957, when Pam gave birth to our daughter, Emma at The Princess Beatrice Hospital in the Old Brompton Road. I remember our stage manager whispering the news to me, while standing in the wings, just before going on stage. After Hurst Lodge School and three years living in Paris, Emma went to The Central School of Speech and Drama. Just as Pam and I were in the same year at the Webber D, Emma was in the same year as her future husband, Rupert Vansittart. But it was not until five years after leaving Central that they met up at a Rodin exhibition and were married within the year, in 1987. She had ten years working as an actress: the Royal Shakespeare Company, *Daisy Pulls It Off* at The Globe, Manchester Royal Exchange and various television roles, before my granddaughters, Loelia and Eden

Robin and Emma
Battersea, 1962

arrived. Emma is also a fine painter and cook. Their home in Fulham is always full of people and laughter. Now that the children are fully fledged, Emma has started working again, for example, playing Rupert's fictional wife in Rowan Atkinson's *Johnny English Reborn*!

My son Robin

Robin was born in 1959 at the Princess Beatrice Hospital, London. His happiest schools were Bodiam and Northease Manor in Sussex. Being a natural cook, he trained to be a chef at Hastings College, going on to work at The Hungry Horse in Fulham Road.

Me, my son Robin Watson and brother Michael Watson

However, he soon got into stage management for, among other companies, the Bubble Theatre on *Return to the Forbidden Planet*. This then led to his following in Emma's footsteps by going to the Central School of Speech and Drama on the acting course. For some years Robin juggled acting with photography, including an archaeological project in Cambodia, as well as living in France for some time.

Robin has found a whole new career in Norwich as a celebrant which involves conducting personalised funerals, weddings and naming ceremonies; a very satisfying job ideally suited to using his training as an actor.

He still does manage to act, though, as well as taking production photographs for the Hostry Festival and the Maddermarket Theatre in Norwich, where he now lives. He he has also recently played Norman in Ronald Harwood's *The Dresser*.

My sister-in law, Patricia Marmont

Pam's older sister, Patricia is known in the family as Pish. A nick name invented by Pam, aged two, while living in Hollywood. After working as an actress, in films such as *Suddenly Last Summer, Helen Of Troy* and *Front Page Story*, she then became a top agent and set up her own company discovering such talents as Kenneth Branagh and Nicholas Hytner.

Grandchildren ....

My daughter, Emma and her husband, Rupert, have two daughters ; Loelia, aged twenty five and Eden aged twenty one. Loelia lives in the Cotswolds with her writer husband, James and their son Hesketh, my first great-grandchild, who is aged 16 months.

Eden is a budding actress and about to play Lady Windermere in *Lady Windermere's Fan* at The Putney Arts Theatre. She will be the fifth generation in the family to go into acting!

My son, Robin has two children, Sam aged twenty, who is just starting his career in the hotel business and, finally, Alicia, aged nine, who will no doubt surprise us all!

Godchildren
I have also been blessed with five Godchildren, Julia Grafton, Joanne Gow, Eleanour Ripman, Lucinda Hanbury and Philip Dundas.

My Brothers, Michael and John
In many ways we three brothers could not have been more different yet so alike physically, to the extent, as I have mentioned before, that Johnnie was often mistaken for me. Sometimes even obliging fans by signing my autograph, rather than explain: "No, so sorry, I'm his brother......."

Johnnie made his career in The Blues and Royals, retiring as a Major, then became sub-editor for Country Life, reporting on all the hunts around The British Isles. He wrote numerous books on fox-hunting, and also history.

Michael started in the army as well, and at the age of 21 was posted off to the South East Asian Command (SEAC) in Singapore under Mountbatten. He was put in charge of collecting evidence to support the War Crime Trials against important Japanese Generals, and was promoted to Major at the incredible age of 22. After demobilisation he returned home to Britain to join the Brewing Company Ind Coope & Allsopp Ltd, ending up in Kenya as MD of all their operations in East Africa. Returning home he then had a great success inventing the boutique style of hotel, running an Award winning, upmarket bed & breakfast in South Kensington called Number Sixteen. It still thrives today..

Kinki
I first met Kinki when I was at The Webber Douglas Academy. Her real name was Lia and she was married to my grandfather, Arthur. Kinki came to live in England from The Black Forest, in Germany in about 1938. Back in Germany, due to being a very close friend of Furtwangler, she found herself socialising with many of the Nazi hierarchy, including Goebbels. She was a very beautiful woman, highly intelligent but also a vocal critic of Nazi policies. Fearing she may be put on a black list, Furtwangler advised her to leave the country until after the ensuing war. So she came to England and in fact never returned to Germany.

Soon after arriving in London, at an Embassy party, knowing no one, she went and introduced herself to my grandfather, Arthur, because he resembled Furtwangler; six foot four and handsome! They were quickly married and enjoyed a very happy twenty years together.

I remember being aware of the awkward situation that my father was going to fight against his new step-mother's country. Indeed she was briefly interned at Holloway Prison as an "Enemy Alien". My grandfather, nick named Lofty, gave her the nickname, Kinki, because of the kink in her hair.

'Kinki' Watson

Arthur Watson

When he died, Kinki invited me to come over and see Arthur's dead body in their flat at Elvaston Place, in Kensington. Never having seen a dead person, I was quite taken aback. But I need not have worried, he looked utterly composed and serene.

Kinki remained a widow, living in London for another 30 years. She was always a delightful, loving and generous spirited step-grandmother to me and my children. I adored her.

Barnes

Pam and I moved from Underwood House to Neaves Park Farm in Hartfield, East Sussex. After eight or so years, in 1992, we realised it was time to move back to London. Our dear friend, Joaquina Howles, recommended Barnes. How right she was!

Pam could walk our beloved golden retriever, Dancer, on the Common, and rekindle lost friendships in town particularly at the increasingly frequent memorial services that we attended at St Paul's, Covent Garden, the actors' church. I could continue doing theatre work without the strain of commuting to and from Sussex. Barnes is stuffed with fellow thespians.

Pam and I with Emma and Robin

Rupert Vansittart, Emma Vansittart with Loelia, Johnnie Watson, Michael Watson, Pam and I (Photograph taken by Robin Watson)

Our house is No 81 and the multi-talented Alistair McGowan lived at No 18 so our post often got muddled up. We became great friends as a result of these mix-ups.

I once took advantage of all this talent living in Barnes and put on a show at St Paul's School to raise a tidy sum for the Tusk and Ackroyd charities. Joining Alistair we had Aled Jones, Patricia Hodge, Michael Ball (guaranteed sell-out!), Edward de Souza, Carolyn Allen, Paul Smith (the musician

With Gyles Brandreth at the Tusk charity event in Barnes

not the designer), Anita Harris, Roger McGough, Gyles Brandreth and Joanna Lumley all doing splendid "turns".

Emma, my daughter, living in Fulham, has often taken me to the Barnes Farmers' Market where we have enjoyed the goodies brought up from as far afield as Somerset and Kent. Yummie vegetables and chicken; thank you Heidi and Andy! My neighbours have sustained me through the transfer to widowhood. There is a fantastic community atmosphere in Barnes. I have so enjoyed my daily routine of walking up our blossom filled road, greeting cherished neighbours on the way to buying my paper.

So easy to potter up to the West End to either meet friends at the Garrick Club or see plays and exhibitions. In order for me to stay in my own home I was fortunate enough to find Danilo to come and live in our spare room. He has kindly prepared me suppers each night while working during the day as a cardiac physiologist at the Charing Cross Hospital.

So now on to a new move....to Denville Hall.

I have hesitated in so many ways going to where many of my friends "end up" partly due to not wanting to be deep in suburbia and away from my beloved home. Now that I am happily settled here in Denville, I have no regrets. It is almost like being on a cruise with, for example, a variety of old and new films being shown almost every day as well as the National Theatre live screenings.

I am surrounded in extraordinary theatrical history not only because of the wonderful theatre memorabilia that fills the house but also re-meeting fellow actors that I worked with decades ago. We are fortunate indeed to have such a haven of familiarity and peace to escape to. I love my room here. The window looks over a beautifully kept garden where I watch the squirrels and birds. The staff are all wonderful.

Also with me is my 94 year old sister-in-law, Patricia Marmont whose own parents, Percy and Dorothy, were here in the 1980s. Dorothy was over 100 when she died at Denville. My old colleagues (Lord) Brian Rix and Philip Grout are also here.

I was born under the sign of Cancer. Our characteristics are apparently well suited to becoming actors. To quote Isabelle M. Pagan, from her book *From Pioneer To Poet*,

> *Cancerians love to come into touch with the public, to claim its interest, to stimulate it's imagination and to sway its moods.*

This has indeed given me great pleasure over the years. To have the audience in the palm of your hand. So looking back on my life, I feel fortunate and grateful for

all the many, varied jobs I have enjoyed. The thrill of a new band of fellow actors. Each show bringing with it a ready-made family. Yes, dropping names here and there, but never dropping friends.

I have been blessed with an extraordinary life. Thank you for sharing this journey with me. I have enjoyed every minute.

Three men arrive at The Pearly Gates to be met by St. Peter.

"What did you do and how much did you earn? " He asks them.

The first man replies:
"I was Chairman of an Insurance Company, grossing about
£200,000 per year."

The second man replies:
"I had a chain of travel agents, and grossed about
£150,000 per year."

The third man says:
"Well, I only worked sporadically......! I suppose I grossed about
£4,000 a year"

St.Peter:-
"REALLY! Might I have seen you in anything?"